THE ESSENTIAL GUIDE TO
Ballroom Dance

THE ESSENTIAL GUIDE TO
Ballroom Dance

JANET CUNNINGHAM-CLAYTON
AND MALCOLM FERNANDES

Foreword by Anton Du Beke

THE CROWOOD PRESS

First published in 2019 by
The Crowood Press Ltd
Ramsbury, Marlborough
Wiltshire SN8 2HR

www.crowood.com

British Library Cataloguing-in-Publication Data
A catalogue record for this book is available from the British Library.

ISBN 978 1 78500 597 8

Typeset by Jean Cussons Typesetting, Diss, Norfolk

Printed and bound in India by Replika Press Pvt Ltd

CONTENTS

FOREWORD *by Anton DuBeke*

PROFESSIONAL DANCER ON THE BBC's *STRICTLY COME DANCING*

Anton DuBeke.

It is a joy to write a foreword to this wonderful book, written by two of my favourite people about my favourite subject matter, ballroom dancing. It is fantastic that here, Janet and Malcolm are able to share their wealth of experience and expertise, amassed over decades at the heart of the industry, that will be invaluable for anyone, wherever they may be on their dancing journey.

I have been lucky enough to know Janet and Malcolm for the past thirty years and we have spent many a happy hour together discussing this wonderful world of ballroom dancing. Anyone that knows me, knows that I have a deep interest in the history of ballroom dancing and its evolution over the past century. From the advent of the professional and amateur championships in the early 1930s to the huge icons of the dancing world from the likes of Phyllis Haylor, Josephine Bradley and Victor Sylvester, to Richard and Janet Cleave and Marcus and Karen Hilton. From the ruthless competition of the professional circuit, the pomp and pageantry of *Come Dancing* to the glitter and glamour of *Strictly Come Dancing* today, it truly is a unique world, which I have been lucky enough to be part of for most of my life.

For the absolute beginner with a passion to learn to dance, to the experienced dancer with a desire to have a greater understanding of the mechanics of the body and to improve technique, this book will be an invaluable companion. It will be taking pride of place on my bookshelf.

ACKNOWLEDGEMENTS

ACKNOWLEDGEMENTS FROM JANET

A life-long thank-you to two very special people in my dancing journey: Peter Elliott, who coached me, helped and encouraged me to 'hold the dream' (his quote); and Scott Draper, who coached me along the road to becoming the British Senior Ballroom Dance Champion and who hung in there with me through all the challenges that occurred along the way.

Many thanks to my practice partner, Donald Knight, who was always there for me to practise with and who was never too busy to help.

Great thanks to my coaches Kenny Welsh, Marion Welsh, David Sycamore, Denise Weavers and Vicky Barr, who, when I was beginning my dancing journey, taught me to aspire to the best technique. Their teaching is what I remember and continue to understand to this day.

Thanks go to my yoga teacher, Sarah Davey-Alexander, for her wonderful teaching abilities and application of the Alexander technique, which has improved my awareness of movement, and my strength and flexibility, as well as my posture, balance and poise. Thank you to my tai chi teachers, Dick Watson and Simon Watson, who trained me in tai chi, which helped me enormously in my dancing, especially in feeling, balance and control.

Thanks to Dick with his quotation of 'you gain by your losses'. I certainly did when losing a partner, then gained Phil Holding with whom I became the British Senior Champion. Thank you Phil.

Thank you too to all the partners that came and went, departing but leaving life-changing lessons.

To my friends John Cremins, Chris Cremins, John Bowyer and Max and Sarah Davis, who all afford me the privilege to teach them and learn even more.

Many, many thanks to my amazing partner in my life Malcolm, Mr Wonderful, who challenged me to teach but who is the most challenging to teach!

ACKNOWLEDGEMENTS FROM MALCOLM

This book would not be on the bookshelf without my partner, mentor and friend Janet. My thanks to Janet for bringing about in me an understanding of ballroom dancing.

Thanks to all the dance promoters who had the faith and belief in me as a dance presenter.

My thanks to all the professional dancers who demonstrated their craft at my social dance balls and who were truly inspirational. Notable amongst these were: Arunas Bizokas and Katusha Demidova; Michael Malitowski and Joanna Leunis; Mirko Gozzoli and Edita Daniute; John Wood and Snieguole Wood; Sergey Surkov and Melia; Paolo Bosco and Silvia Pitton; Vincent Simone and Flavia Cacace; Warren and Kristi Boyce; Pablo Alonso and Caro; and to the many amateur couples who were also inspirational.

SPECIAL THANKS FROM MALCOLM AND JANET

Our special thanks and gratitude to the talented photographer, Fredric Frennessen, for his skill and patience and the splendid photographs in this book.

Vicki Frennessen, thank you for Janet's hairstyle and make-up, and your assistance in our poses for the photographs.

Shermain Philip, thank you for all your hard work creating the wonderful illustrations in this book.

Thank you to Ronnie Li and Sylvie Morton of Chrisanne Clover for the beautiful dance dresses worn by Janet and photographed in this book.

Thank you to Gerald Schwanzer of Dance Sport International London for the practice wear worn by Janet in the dance step photographs, and the peach ballroom dress worn by Janet in the book.

Thank you to Espen Salberg for your kind and helpful advice and the beautiful black evening dress like the one shown in the book worn by Janet.

Thank you to SupaDance International for the dance shoes as worn by Janet and me in the photographs.

Our special thanks to Steve, Sam and Pauline at WRD Records for consistently providing Malcolm with the best dance CDs.

PREFACE

Janet and I found our way into the ballroom dancing world via two entirely different routes.

Janet's route was the more conventional of the two and is the one that will be familiar to hundreds of young girls and ladies throughout the world who have taken up ballroom dancing.

Like so many young girls, she was encouraged by her parents to learn to dance and was enrolled into one of the many 'Victor Silvester Dance Schools' abounding in London, this one being in Kilburn High Road. She was eight years old at the time. She then went through several years of dance lessons taking her medal examinations and finally attaining Gold Star status and Statuette. She remembers being presented her many medal awards by Lionel Blair, Judith Chalmers and Bruce Forsythe – days that are etched in her memory.

Janet sadly stopped dancing when she was twenty to follow a full-time career working with horses, and resumed her dancing many years later. Her interest was rekindled through watching the BBC's *Come Dancing* programmes on television. She was enthralled watching the wonderful Shirley Ballas dancing with her husband Corky, performing the Samba to the Samuel E. Wright song *Under the Sea*. She was also inspired by the Finnish professional dancers Sirpa Suutari and Jukka Haapalainen, and the British dancers Barbara McColl and Sammy Stopford.

She joined a local dance school in Watford, England and once again enjoyed inter-school competitions with her dance teacher. Her aim then was to dance on the British competitive dance circuit and her dream was to become the British Senior Ballroom Champion. She was encouraged in

Janet Cunningham-Clayton.

this goal by one of her early coaches, Peter Elliot, who frequently told her to 'hold the dream' when times were proving to be difficult. She soon found her first dancing partner, Don Knight, to practise with, which led her on to finding her first competitive dancing partner. As well as continuing her lessons with her coach, she started having lessons with other top coaches.

After the breakup of her first partnership, she travelled the length and breadth of England, and even abroad as far away as Australia, in her search for a dance partner. She was finally introduced to home-grown Phil Holding, with whom she finally achieved her goal, in 2007, of winning the British Senior Ballroom Championship in Blackpool, England. She also achieved eighteenth place in the World Senior Standard Championship at Antwerp in February 2008.

She talks of the constant support given to her by her dance coaches, on her long and truly enlightening journey. She often quotes an anonymous author:

Malcolm Fernandes.

Pupil, 'Is the road uphill all of the way?'
Teacher, 'Yes, all the way to the very top.'

She would like to add here the beneficial help she attained from her yoga teacher Sarah Davey-Alexander and her tai chi teachers who she refers to as also being instrumental in her success as a ballroom dancer.

Her motto has been: To have a meaningful journey you have to embrace everything – mind, body and soul.

You need your Mind to be able to assimilate information.
You need your Body to be able to perform it.
And you also need your Soul to be able feel it.

After retiring from the competitive dance circuit, she fatefully met me on the London social dance scene and on our first meeting on the dance floor, surprised me when she said that she so enjoyed dancing with me that first time and had a lot of fun. She said my dancing was soft, free and untamed.

I, on the other hand, couldn't dance a step at that time. I had not had any formal, or indeed informal, dance lessons up until then and I immediately soaked up all the knowledge, information, teaching and instruction that she subsequently gave me, for which I will be forever grateful.

As I was, by then, not only hosting social ballroom dances but also organizing dance holidays and associated dance workshops, I suggested that she might consider taking dance teaching examinations and qualifying as a dance instructor, so that she could undertake the workshops on my holidays. This she did and she is now a qualified dance teacher.

My love of dance arose from my love of music. My love of music, I suppose, started when I was still an infant. I was told by my mother that before I was one year old she used to take me to dances with my father back home in Kenya. I used to be put in my Moses basket on the side of the stage while my father played guitar and my mother danced the night away. Although I didn't have any ability to play music, albeit a desire to do so, I always aspired to be some kind of performer and to be on a stage.

I arrived in the UK from Kenya in 1968 with this vision to be a performer still burning. I went through school and college, and started my working life still not knowing how to realize my ambition. It was purely by chance that, in 1979, a friend of mine, knowing that I had a huge record collection, asked me to bring them along and play them at a local youth club event that he was organizing. That night is indelibly stamped in my memory. With one record player connected to a pair of speakers I engaged with the dancers, and my ability to play and present music that made people want to dance was awakened. I realized then that what I wanted to do was host public dances.

People seemed to like my style and I began getting lots of work everywhere, hosting weddings, parties and corporate events. That was the wonderful era of disco and people were dancing to the music of the Bee Gees, Gloria Gaynor and Earth, Wind and Fire. It was at one of these events that another DJ asked me to cover one of his regular engagements at the famous 'Café de Paris' in London's Leicester Square. I didn't know it at the time, but the Café de Paris was run by the Mecca Leisure Group and was then one of the last bastions of ballroom dancing still remaining in London. In November 1987, I hosted my first tea dance inside this beautiful dance hall with absolutely no idea of what ballroom dancing was all about.

The first thing I noticed, with absolute amazement, was that no sooner had the doors opened, than the people rushed down the beautiful iconic double staircase, put on their dance shoes and stepped out on to the dance floor, as soon as I struck up the first dance.

The second thing I noticed that afternoon was that these people were actually 'dancing'. They seemed to know what they were doing and their feet appeared to be dancing predetermined steps. The men appeared to be 'leading' their partners and the ladies seemed to know what the men were doing and could 'follow' them. It must be said that this was my first introduction to hosting a ballroom event. It was on one such occasion that a very nice lady said, smilingly, to me, 'That was wonderful dancing! You are Mr Wonderful'; and my stage name was born. I fell in love with this 'new' kind of social dancing.

Soon after that, I was being asked to host ballroom dances all over London. I quit my job, and my career as a professional dance presenter began. From then on, it has been my privilege to host ballroom dances in all the major dance halls in London and other cities in the UK. It has also been my pleasure to bring top class professional and amateur world champion dancers to perform at my social dances and balls. It was at one of these social dances that I met Janet, the lady who was destined to become my girlfriend, partner and mentor. I had no idea at that time that she was a former British Senior Ballroom Dance Champion. She began teaching me the techniques of ballroom dancing, of which I had no idea, moulding and forming me into a dancer.

INTRODUCTION

Ballroom dancing has many benefits to offer those wishing to take up this very popular pastime. Some of these many benefits are the social ones – making new friends and attending social dances and enjoying the company of friends in a convivial atmosphere.

Dancing on a regular basis will tone and strengthen the muscles, and generally increase overall fitness and aid weight loss. It is also a weight-bearing, bone-loading exercise, which helps prevent osteoporosis. It will also improve lung capacity and increase stamina, as it is a cardiovascular exercise. It will challenge the mental faculties through learning and subsequently remembering new steps and routines. New research has shown that it has a capacity of delaying the onset of dementia and even Alzheimer's disease. Many take their dancing further and take medal examinations, which are both challenging and rewarding.

Passion for dancing may have been fuelled by watching one of the many reality programmes on the television or through seeing one of the many ballroom dancing movies, which sparked a yearning to learn to dance. Whatever the reasons for choosing to enter this wonderful world of ballroom dancing, dancing will bring you all the above benefits and a lot of fun as well!

This book has been mapped out in a way that should be easy for the reader to follow. By following this map from start to finish, without any deviation, the reader should gain a good understanding of how to dance and be able to become a competent ballroom dancer.

We begin with the history and development of ballroom dancing from its earliest inception to what is happening in the dance world today. It includes a basic understanding of music, in relatively simple terms, to make it easy to comprehend, giving an understanding of the relationship between music and the dance steps. Detailed explanations of dancing terms and techniques, including deportment – both individually and as a couple – are covered. The beginner steps of all the five dances are explained in detail to give you the confidence to step out on to any dance floor. This is followed by an introduction to more advanced choreography and techniques that will increase your repertoire of dance steps and how to dance them to a higher standard.

The book aims not only to cover 'steps' but to give the reader the knowledge of movement to enable them to dance these steps. This is absolutely vital in becoming a proficient dancer.

At the end of the book, there are exercises that have been recommended to increase your core strength and improve your flexibility and mobility.

The experienced dancer may benefit by finding that the information in this book will supplement and reinforce their knowledge and experience, and help them to develop their own dancing ability further.

If, after reading this book, you develop a passion for ballroom dancing, we suggest ways that will enable you to take your dancing further.

The steps have been deliberately kept as simple as possible, as the book aims to enable the new dancer to work on the fundamentals and foundations that will allow them to dance correctly from the very beginning, so as not to have to break bad habits further along the road that can be

Ballroom should be an enjoyable journey.

caused by trying to dance advanced choreography too soon.

Learning to dance the steps correctly is vital to be able to perform the dance well. Improper actions will result in bad dancing. This can be likened to making a successful sponge cake, where the right ingredients in the correct amounts, baked at the correct temperature and for the right duration of time, must be adhered to. It is important to mix the ingredients in a specific way for the sponge to turn out perfect.

This will make the difference between an average and very good sponge cake.

An unknown author quotes: 'countless unseen details are often the only difference between mediocre and magnificent'.

The key to successful dancing is to gain the knowledge of how to dance correctly, and many hours of practice.

So now let's begin and enjoy the journey!

CHAPTER 1

THE HISTORY AND DEVELOPMENT OF BALLROOM DANCING

From the dawn of humanity, humankind has been dancing:

- Cave paintings have depicted early people dancing.
- There are even hieroglyphics of people dancing on the walls of Egyptian tombs.
- Native American Indians danced to bring on the rains.
- The African Maasai people danced to demonstrate their sexual prowess.
- Samoans danced to frighten off their enemies.
- Japanese geisha women danced to entertain their male customers.

Dancing has been the mainstay of human social behaviour since the beginning of human history. Today, there are myriad styles of dance ranging from baton twirling to line dancing to synchronized swimming. In this book, we are going to introduce you to the joy of modern ballroom dancing, sometimes called the International Style of ballroom dancing. If you are new to ballroom dancing, your journey will begin here!

The word 'ballroom' originates from the Latin word 'ballare' a word that means 'to dance' and so the word ballroom presumably means a room where people come together to dance. The first annotated description of early ballroom dancing can be traced to around the sixteenth century. Towards the end of the seventeenth century, a simple choreography of dances was beginning to be written down and annotated.

It has been suggested that the classic ballroom hold that we see today originated at a time when men were regaled with their swords dangling on their left sides and so, to keep the lady's arm away from the sword, the man would hold her left hand with his right hand at shoulder level away from the sword.

The waltz is undoubtedly the first and original of all the ballroom dances. In the nineteenth century, it began to become popularized in England. It developed from the European waltz (now referred to as the Viennese waltz), which was danced at a much faster pace by the folk people of Germany and Austria. The 'English waltz' or 'classical waltz' that we dance today, developed much later, around the 1920s, in – as you would guess – England! At first, this slower 'English waltz' met with huge indignation and opposition by society because of the scandalous proximity of the couple and the close hold of the man and woman, which was thought, at the time, to be rather improper, immoral and, indeed, shameful. Eventually, as morals softened, modern ballroom dancing began to evolve and develop. All this was socially engineered from the top of the social strata, downwards. The upper class were dancing at their 'society balls' and top hotels had their own resident orchestras playing dance music. Indeed, Queen Victoria and Prince Albert had a penchant for ballroom dancing. So, if it was seen to be good enough for the 'upper classes', it was good enough for the rest of society.

Dancing consequently became a very popular and relaxing social pastime. People spent their hard-earned money in newly built dance halls. These were the places that people went to meet and socialize together. This, in turn, increased the need for dance bands and orchestras, which, in turn, led to the 'invention' and 'creation' of newer and newer dances for people to enjoy. Dance fever erupted and dance halls opened up all over Britain, North America and Europe.

In the early 1920s, people like Victor Silvester in Britain began to clarify, theorize, formalize and standardize, and began teaching these dances. Silvester was a London-based professional dancer and won the first ballroom dancing championship in 1922 with his partner Phyllis Clarke. He is credited with the 'invention' of the full natural turn and the double reverse spin in the waltz. He was a founder member of the Imperial Society of Teachers of Dancing (ISTD) and he went on to open a chain of Dance Academies in London.

As a dancer, he was unashamedly aware that the bands and orchestras of the time did not offer the correct timing and tempos in the music they played that dancers required and demanded. He consequently formed his own five-piece band to provide this 'strict tempo dance music'. He started laying down musical arrangements that were driven by the strict timing of the metronome. He later enlarged his band to form the 'Victor Silvester Orchestra', which he later further augmented by adding a comprehensive string ensemble for BBC radio broadcasts and called 'The Silver Strings'. He is reputed to have achieved record sales of 75 million from the 1930s through to the 1980s.

As the popularity of dancing increased, more and more people wanted to learn to dance – dance schools abounded and dancing was exported to all parts of the Western world. All of this was happening in the era before the invention and arrival of television. Dancing at that time formed the major part of the Western world's social scene. People met at dance halls and fell in love there.

To a large extent, the invention and spread of television killed off social dancing, as people began to stay indoors rather than go out to dance. Ironically, it now appears that with the revival of various dance programmes on TV today, ballroom dancing is making a resurgence all over the world. Coupled to this, there have been several hugely entertaining box-office hit movies featuring Hollywood stars that have tempted people back to dance halls and inspired people to learn to dance.

Notable among these are:

- The 1992 Australian romantic comedy *Strictly Ballroom* starring Paul Mercurio and directed and co-written by Baz Luhrmann. 2018 has seen it brought to the stage on Broadway and London.
- The 2004 American remake of the Japanese award-winning film of the same name, *Shall We Dance*, starring Richard Gere and Jennifer Lopez.
- The 2006 *Take the Lead* starring Antonio Banderas as dance instructor Pierre Dulaine.

The ballroom dancing craze, which had its advent in the West, now appears to be sweeping across the globe. The former Philippine Senator Rene Saguisag described ballroom dancing: 'It is exquisite!' and 'It is good clean fun, and we have lost a lot of weight!' When General Alfredo Filler of the country's armed forces was asked at his retirement what he wanted to do for the rest of his life, he is reputed to have said, 'I want to learn ballroom dancing.'

In mainland China, people are now replacing their tai chi routine by practising their ballroom steps in the early morning parks of Beijing and Shanghai Bund. It even comes with dim sum in Hong Kong restaurants.

Millions of people have found the ballroom bug in Japan. It is not unusual for middle-aged and elderly women to leave their husbands at work while they tango and foxtrot away in the afternoons.

In Singapore, ballroom dancing has been added to activities like tennis and wine-tasting events and is now government funded.

Dancing in Australia was brought in by the British Colonial settlers. As they settled in the small towns all over the continent, dancing was their only form of entertainment. Indeed, in many of the outback towns there are still old dance halls used for social dances. The Australians have developed their own style of sequence dancing called 'new vogue', which has its roots in ballroom dancing figures.

The dance craze is giving birth to an expanding new profession of dance instructor and professional dance partner, who are mainly young, attractive, athletic males. They service the new Pro Am market, where they partner their students in exotic locations like Bali, Dubai and Milan.

People all over the world today are getting off their couches and heading to dance schools or dance halls to enjoy partner dancing again!

Reality television dance programmes now feature all over the world. Based on the British TV show *Strictly Come Dancing*, the format has been successfully licensed to a multitude of countries across the globe. The shows pair off well-known celebrities with professional ballroom dancers who compete against each other; their dancing is then judged by a panel of experts and subsequently voted on by the watching public to ultimately produce a winning couple.

Countries now broadcasting the franchised show include Argentina, Australia, Brazil, China (including mainland Hong Kong), Colombia, Germany, India, Indonesia, Japan, South Korea, Pakistan, Peru, Russia, Sweden, Turkey, Ukraine and the United States, with more countries broadcasting it every year.

CHAPTER 2

THE DANCE ESSENTIALS

DANCE ATTIRE

Dance attire is different from everyday clothes. Wearing the right clothes will make dancing easier and more comfortable, enabling freedom of movement, while wearing any tight-fitting clothes will restrict your ability to move.

Men should wear light, fitted trousers and a shirt with sleeves worn over a vest to absorb perspiration.

Ladies should not restrict their movement by wearing tight-fitting skirts, as the man will not be able to walk forward inside the lady's leg. Tight-fitting tops will also restrict the lady in her hold. Specialized dance wear takes all of this into consideration. Ladies should also wear correctly fitting

Dance attire skirt and top shown in dance material that breathes, suitable for dancing.

Ladies' dance shoes shown with a heel protector.

Ladies' dance shoes with suede soles, which are available from special dance-wear suppliers.

dancing shoes with suede soles and the appropriate heel height. This will make the dancing more enjoyable.

Dance wear can be obtained from a specialized dance-wear shop, which has a variety of dance-wear clothes that are designed to give maximum freedom to move and are made with a suitable fabric that breathes and draws moisture from the body, where it can evaporate more easily. This will also prevent perspiration marks from forming.

Comfortable dance shoes, preferably with suede soles, should also be worn. It is advisable to buy dance shoes from reputable dance-wear suppliers because this will help you in many ways. Dance shoes are made to prevent damaging dance floors and to help prevent slipping and falling. Heel protectors can also be worn to prevent the heels of shoes wearing down very quickly. Normal outdoor shoes are not really suitable for dancing because most of them do not have non-slip soles and can be heavy. Stiletto heels are not very appropriate and will damage dance floors.

Please also remember your basic hygiene regime, as dancing is performed in close contact with your partner.

Men's patent dance
shoes, with suede
soles.

THE MUSIC

It is necessary to have a basic understanding of music, because music is, ultimately, the tool that dancers perform with. Without music, dancing would seem very bland. As dancers, we interpret the dance through the music, as well as expressing the character of the dance.

Today the world is blessed in having, through digital media, compact discs, vinyl records and even live orchestras and dance bands, access to a huge wealth of dance music. Inspired composers, skilful arrangers and talented musicians all conspire to bring to our ears the music that inspires us to dance.

What Exactly Is Music?

Essentially, music can be defined as a series of sounds that are laid down by musicians in a prede-termined way to form a musical melody. These musical melodies are measured in beats and bars, and together they are called 'time signatures'. In the waltz, for example, this is stated as being in 3/4 time, meaning that there are three beats to each bar of music, having a tempo of between 28 and 30 bars per minute.

Both the foxtrot and quickstep are arranged and

The music.

played in 4/4 timing meaning that there are 4 beats to each bar. So although both of these dances share the same time signature, the difference between the two dances lies in the tempo or speed in which these melodies are played. Foxtrot is played at 30–32 bars per minute, while the quickstep is played at around 50 bars per minute. Tango is played in 2/4 or 4/4 timing and has a usual tempo of 33 bars per minute. The Viennese waltz is played in 3/4 time at a tempo of between 50 and 60 bars per minute.

Whatever the dance, it is important that the speed or timing of the music remains constant throughout. This is often referred to as 'strict tempo' music.

HOW TO STAND CORRECTLY

Before taking the first dance step, learning how to stand correctly and on our own balance must be achieved. In dancing this is referred to as posture and poise. Standing on balance, on first thought, might seem to be very easy to achieve, but it takes time and practice to perfect. When watching good dancers, they will have mastered the three elements of balance, posture and poise.

The illustration demonstrates four incorrect standing positions and the fifth figure is the correct position.

Balance

Balance is the most important and essential necessity in dancing. Without balance, you will not be able to dance correctly or comfortably. There are two types of balance: static and dynamic balance.

Consider this: if an object is dropped from the

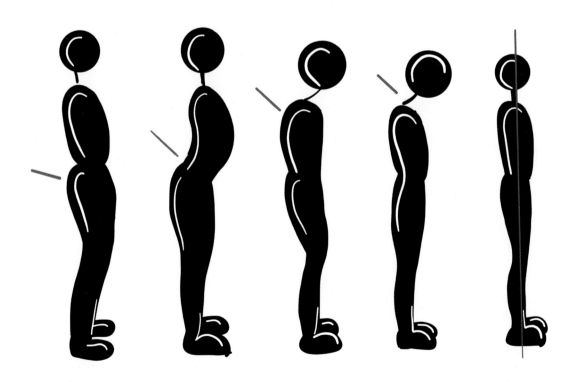

How to stand – first four stick men show an incorrect posture; the fifth stick man shows the correct posture.

hand, it would naturally fall straight down to the ground because of the force of gravity acting on it pulling it downwards. The object would not veer to the left or to the right or backwards or forward – it would fall straight down.

When dancing, we need to be aware that gravity is also acting on our bodies, pulling the body weight downwards and, although we are seldom aware of this, the body is constantly fighting against this downward pull to stay upright.

Try this out to feel how gravity affects us. Stand straight and sway to the side or to the back or to the front – gravity will want to make us tip over in the direction of the weight load and it is only the combined action of our muscles exerting an equal force in the opposite direction that will prevent us from falling over.

In dancing, constant attention is put into maintaining the centre of gravity of the body when moving. There is a constant striving to stay on balance without using forced muscle strength and, consequently, saving energy and thus dancing efficiently and comfortably. There is, therefore, a need for the weight to be dropping down through the spine vertically.

Balance will be achieved when we are standing in a proper vertical stance with the head directly aligned over the spine and the body weight falling downwards through the spine from the head, through the shoulders, ribcage and hips to the ankles and feet. This allows the weight to be evenly distributed for the minimal amount of stress on the spine, so that when standing still, you are prevented from falling over.

To further illustrate this, refer to the image on the previous page and look at the fifth figure. Imagine a pole that goes straight down through the centre of the body similar to the spine; the pole has to stay vertical to the floor. Bending to the side would create a weight load that would cause a fall to that side. The same would happen if bending backwards or forward – the shifting of the weight would pull the body in that direction.

There should be no feeling of the body being carried upwards by using the muscles. The shoulders should be pulling down the back, which causes the chest to rise slightly in an upward direction. Do not try to force the chest upwards as this will result in concaving the back and a feeling that the weight is being carried upwards. It is the use of our legs that support our bodies in an upward direction. When dancing, the aim should be to maintain this state of balance.

When we dance, we have to maintain a balance between the couple to enable the partnership to dance together. We therefore need to change weight at the same time, and any pulling or pushing of each other will create a bumping action, so it is very important for both partners to be on their own balance. This will be explained in detail in Chapter 7 (*see* section Balance in More Detail).

It is often said that the most important thing in dancing is to dance in time to the music. Dancing in time to the music can only be achieved by acquiring good balance. Having good balance gives us the control of our body that we require to be able to perform a correct action in transferring our weight from one foot to the other foot, thereby allowing us to dance in time.

Posture

Posture in dancing is defined as the proper positioning of all the parts of the body in a vertical alignment. It is this proper lining up of all these parts that enables the skeletal system to hold the body upright against the downward pull of gravity. The spine is made up of five sections (from top to bottom): cervical, thoracic, lumbar, sacrum and coccyx. The sacrum and coccyx are fixed together in a single bone that cannot move independently. The lumbar spine is the lower back and naturally curves back. The thoracic spine, which extends approximately from the lower ribs to the bottom of the neck, naturally curves forward. The cervical spine extends through the neck to end below the ears, and naturally curves back. Exaggeration of any of these parts will cause bad posture and the appearance of a shortening and collapsing of the spine. This is often seen in dancing and is incorrect as the dancer needs to stretch the spine and not collapse it. When

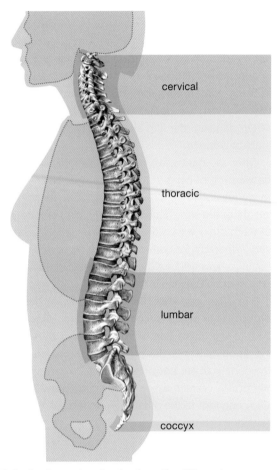

Spinal column drawing to show the different sections of the spine that are discussed in this chapter. WILLIAM CROCHOT/WIKIMEDIA

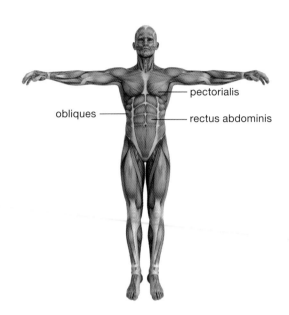

Rectus abdominis, obliques and pectoralis muscles discussed in this chapter. SHUTTERSTOCK

the curves of the spine are lengthened, a taller and more projected upward look is achieved.

The whole spine must be balanced and any distortion of any of these parts, causing the spine to be out of line, will upset the posture. For example, throwing the head back or pushing the stomach out or throwing a hip out will result in an incorrect dance posture. Posture can be considered to be the lengthening of the spine. How do we achieve this without becoming stiff and using a lot of force to stand tall?

Lengthening the spine can be achieved by dropping the tail bone, which means moving the coccyx towards the floor. Also, trying to pull the belly button

to the back of the spine will give a feeling of the lower back lengthening. To stretch the thoracic spine, try to push the back of the spine to the front of the spine (this stretches the rectus adominis muscles known as the six-pack) and obtain a feeling of the shoulder blades coming together and the chest plate rising upwards and shoulders pulling downwards.

The head should sit so that it looks as if half is in front of shoulders and half behind the shoulders. If the neck is too far forward, it is because the thoracic spine is being curved or rounded beyond its natural curve, causing the head to drop forward. Trying to lift the head or straighten the neck will not correct the problem, as this is not normally the cause. The thoracic spine is maybe where the problem lies and this needs to be worked on to correct the over-curvature of this area.

The spinal column is made up of bone and cannot operate on its own, it is the combination of the spine with the muscles in our back that creates good posture, and we need to be able to use them correctly; some muscles need to be engaged and some need to be stretched. The erector spinae muscles run down both sides of the spine and they

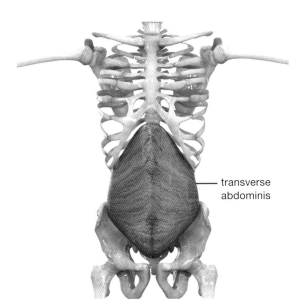

— transverse abdominis

Transverse abdominis. SHUTTERSTOCK

connect the ribs to the vertebrae; when they are tightened, the chest expands and the curve in the thoracic spine will decrease.

Other muscles that we use are the transverse abdominis muscles beneath all the other abdominal muscles. They wrap around the trunk from front to back and provide support similar to a corset or girdle. When they are contracted, it feels as if you are pulling your belly button and the sides of the body inwards, making you grow upwards and the hips feel as though they are pushing downwards. Engaging these muscles also prevents over-extension of the lower back and a look of pushing the stomach out as it holds the lower ribs down.

The abdominal muscles known as the 'six pack' are the rectus abdominis and these muscles need to stretch; tightening them will cause you to crunch up. If done correctly, the upper spine will extend and the hips will push down.

The big and small muscles of the chest are the pectoralis major and minor; these muscles must not be tightened and should stretch also. If they are tight, they can cause the chest to cave inwards and stop the stretch from chest to collarbone.

A lengthened spine will help you look taller and will project you upwards.

Trying to pull the shoulders back will create tension. Try instead to move the shoulders away from each other and fold the shoulder blades in. As you move the shoulders away from each other, you might find that the shoulder blades naturally fold in. Try to keep the neck soft as you do this.

To be efficient in movement, the spine must not be braced, as this works against easy movement. Try to identify where you may be stiffening and holding tension in the body, and try to use the muscles correctly.

Ladies' Extension

The lady's posture when extending the dancing hold as a couple and extension in the posture when dancing figures called lines.

The lady has to develop her posture to a greater degree. When extending the muscles that are previously been mentioned have to be engaged more and the ones that were described as stretched have to be stretched even further.

When extending in line figures, the lower back should not be compressed by leaning backwards from the waist and concaving the spine. The neck should remain stretched. The chest is spread through the pectoralis major and minor and the front (rectus abdominis) is stretched through the whole front. The core (transverse abdominis) is maintained. When trying to emulate top dancers that you may see, try to remember the fundamentals in this chapter to avoid an unsightly and incorrect look by leaning backwards from the lower back, which can pull the partnership off-balance and can also damage the spine.

Exercise for Improving Posture

The following exercise will help with achieving a good posture at all times.

Stand up against a wall with the head backing on to the wall and the eyes looking forward. Line up the back of the head, the shoulders, hips and the heels against the wall. Start by stretching the neck upwards with the chin tucked in. Do not lift the chin as this will shorten the back of the neck. Pull the shoulders down the back. Pull the navel to the back of the spine and feel the spine lengthening. Keep the knees slightly flexed and not locked. Think of the spine being pulled from both ends: the neck part being pulled up from the back of the head and the tail-bone part being pulled down. At the same time, push the balls of the feet into the floor and take the front of the thigh to the back of the thigh. Try not to stand stiff.

Having done this correctly, and with regular practice, good posture can be achieved. Having an incorrect posture will not only result in being off-balance, but will also put a strain on the whole body and will also affect the partner's balance, putting a strain on his or her body at the same time. Bad posture can result in muscle aches and, at worst,

even injury, as the body has to overcompensate to recover its balance.

Having a strong core will help towards having good posture; it is the abdominal muscles and the muscles that wrap around the mid-section that should be strengthened. The aim of the dancer should be to develop this area. Suggestions for exercises to increase core strength can be found in Chapter 9.

Poise

Figure showing poise and a vertical stance.

The dictionary defines poise as 'the bearing or deportment of the head and body' and in dancing it refers to the 'pitch of the body and placement of the body weight relative to the feet'.

The head weighs approximately between 5 and 11lb (2.25 and 5kg), so what the head is doing affects our balance. Standing in a correct vertical stance, the head will be aligned directly over the spine creating a central point of balance from head to foot and there will be minimal strain on the spine. Anything that is done with the head can upset this balance point. So as a dancer, this alignment of the head and spine has to be maintained while moving and making shapes with the body. Using the head incorrectly will affect dancing in a negative way. For example, trying to pivot or spin with the head tipped or tilted will unbalance the dancer and the couple. A common mistake made by beginner dancers is to look down at their feet to see what their feet are doing; this stops the dancer feeling what the body is doing, so try not to develop this habit as it may be hard to break later on. Head weight is explained in more detail in Chapter 7.

At the start of a dance, the man should stand upright with his body weight held between the feet and the weight falling downwards towards the balls of the feet. The knees should be slightly flexed. The lady should also stand vertically upright with her knees slightly flexed. The body weight should be over the balls of the feet. The lady's poise in dancing will be explained in Chapter 7.

When dancing, the body position will constantly change as movement occurs. Having the right poise helps to maintain balance and shape while moving.

Good dancing is a combination of good balance, posture and poise.

A STEP

When we dance, our ears hear the beats of the music and we move to the sounds of these beats. In ballroom dances (as opposed to Latin American dances) we dance on the first beat of the bar.

When dancing (hopefully, in time to the music), a series of steps are essentially being taken in time to the music that is being listened to.

What Is Meant by a Step?

A step occurs when making a complete change of body weight from one foot to the other. This is another very important idea to understand.

When taking a step, the whole of the body weight will be transferred from one foot to the other foot. A step is not completed until all of the body weight is transferred from the standing foot to the moving one, which then becomes the next standing foot. If the weight is not completely on one foot or the other, then the step has not been completed. When the weight is in between the feet, the step still has not been completed.

The steps that are danced can be either slow or quick. When dancing a slow step in foxtrot and quickstep, two beats of music are taken up and when dancing steps that are referred to as a quick, only one beat of music is taken up. However, in the tango, the slow step is taken up by one beat and the quick is half a beat. In the waltz, one beat to one step is used, unless using syncopation when there are more than three steps danced in only three beats. In syncopation steps, the time is used from the previous beat or the following beat, so time is stolen from a whole beat. For example, Figures danced to the count of I & 2, 3 would be made up of four steps but would only take up three beats of music and not four. Time is taken from beat 1 or 2 to allow for the & count, enabling four steps to be danced in three beats of music that make up one bar.

At this point, it is very important to mention that to dance correctly and comfortably with a partner, it is essential to recognize that the step that is being taken has derived from the one previously danced and it will lead on to the one that will follow. Only by performing every step correctly is it possible to dance well, both individually and with a partner. This will be discussed further in the beginner technique in Chapter 2 (Dance Essentials) and the advanced technique in Chapter 7 (Beyond the Basics), under the heading of forward and backward walks. It will also be referred to under the heading of

Drawing showing the correct action of the legs when transferring weight while walking.

first place. This is attested to by people who have had leg injuries having to learn to walk again.

Concentrating on the actual mechanics of walking nearly always brings about an awareness that makes it apparent that some walking actions are incorrect. Think of the finishing school for girls and how they used to balance books on their heads to have a good deportment. Now, by trying this exercise, it could bring about a realization of walking in an entirely different way. Becoming more conscious of finding a balance and keeping your body still so as not to let a book fall off your head, is what you are trying to achieve in dancing, so that there is a constant awareness of where the balance is.

Now, try to do this same exercise walking forward and backwards. Trying this exercise with a book on the head can be very useful in showing up any incorrect and unnecessary movements.

transference of weight in the forward and backward walks in Chapter 7.

So, now having an understanding of the music and how to step in time to the music, it is almost time to step out on to the dance floor.

The most important movements to start off with are the forward and backward walks. These walks should be studied and learnt well as they will be the foundations of your dancing.

Have you ever thought that the way you walk might be preventing you from moving well?

THE FORWARD WALK

It is natural to think that walking properly and correctly happens naturally and automatically and it is not necessary to break it down and analyse its mechanics, but this is not the case, as a degree of concentration is necessary to be able to perform a good walking action.

We learn to walk as babies after taking a few tumbles and then it appears that we 'forget' how we learnt to walk, or indeed how we stay upright in the

Middle position demonstrated in a dance step showing the weight held between the feet.

Start with the walk forward: standing as straight as possible, while balancing a book on your head, start with the right leg, which is the standing leg, and have all the weight on this leg. Now move the weight very slowly from the heel of the foot towards the ball of the foot and feel the centre of gravity start to move. It will feel as though the base or pelvis has started to move forward and the right knee and shin bone are starting to lower slightly towards the floor. At the same time, the left knee is starting to rise and the ball of the foot will be skimming the floor as it starts to move in a forward direction. Now the left leg will start to move in front of the right, still skimming the floor with the ball of the foot. Continue to roll the weight through the ball of the right foot and the left foot will strike the floor with the heel. Now, standing on the ball of the right foot and the heel of the left foot, you should be in a split leg position, which is sometimes referred to as the middle position.

If this position is bypassed and the body and head start to fall forward causing the weight to fall, the book will most likely fall off your head. Having put the left toe down, continue moving the base forward (the pelvis area, as described below, and in more detail in Chapter 7), and not the top part of your body, the chest area and the head; move completely on to your left leg by moving the base and flexing the left knee. As this happens, the right foot peels off the floor by continuing the rolling action of the foot. It is important that there is no pushing out of the right foot, as this will cause the body to be catapulted forward; let the foot peel off the floor naturally. The right foot will now skim the floor on the ball of the foot to close to the left foot.

The base is the lower part of the body from the hips to the feet. In dancing we use this term so the dancer learns to use the hips and bottom and tops of the legs, rather than throw the body forward from the chest and head.

Demonstration of the positions danced through in the forward walk.

Demonstration of incorrect posture while dancing the forward walk.

When commencing to lower through the legs try not to let the body collapse and the head fall forward as this is incorrect, and will also unbalance you.

THE BACKWARD WALK

Standing on the right foot start to move the hips backwards, as if there was a seat to sit on about a foot away; this moves the centre of the body. There is a feeling of rolling the weight from the ball of the foot to the heel. Do not start the movement by leaning backwards with the head and shoulders. Do not go in a downward direction, as if in a lift. When starting to move backwards, the left foot should be in a position ready to move backwards on the toe, skimming the floor until the foot is in position to receive the weight when it rolls on to the ball of the foot. This is now the middle position, where the front foot is on a heel and the back foot is on a ball; having reached this split leg position, the weight is now evenly distributed between the feet. Move the base so as to transfer the weight by slightly flexing the knee of the back leg and straighten the knee of

Demonstration of the positions danced through in the backward walk.

the front leg, while releasing the right foot from the floor. The heel of the left foot will lower to the floor as the right foot comes into the side of the left foot and the heel must not lower before. The right foot should skim the floor on the ball of the foot on its way into the left foot. The core muscles are used to carry out this action. Movement is initiated from the base through the legs, and not through the body. It is very important that the back heel lowers very slowly and with control.

The illustrations will show a deeper lowering than that which would be expected from a beginner dancer, so try not to worry about a deep lowering action at this stage in the dancing.

At this point, having mastered the forward and backward walks individually, these walks can now be practised together with a partner in the ballroom dancer's hold.

ATTAINING THE BALLROOM DANCER'S HOLD

Note that the following description of the ballroom dancer's hold applies to the waltz, foxtrot, quickstep and Viennese waltz. The tango hold is different and will be explained in Chapter 6.

ABOVE: **Ballroom hold. How to position the arms when taking up the ballroom hold from the man's perspective.**

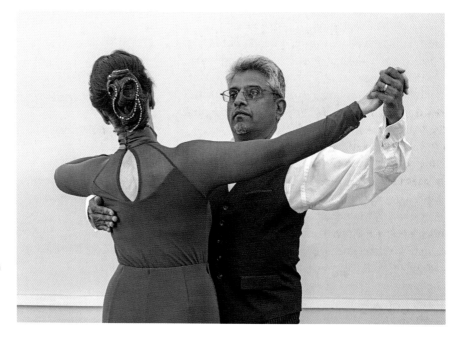

Ballroom hold. How to position the arms when taking up the ballroom hold from the lady's perspective.

Stand as tall as possible, without stretching or feeling uncomfortable. Have a feeling of the lower half of the body pushing down into the floor and the upper body pulling in an upward direction. Keep in mind the previous paragraphs on posture. Lift the ribcage and have the weight of the body falling through the spine to the feet. Pull the shoulders down your back, with the shoulder blades inwards and not stretched apart.

The lady now steps forward towards the man and takes his left hand with her right hand. It is important to note here that neither the man nor the lady should grip the hand of their partner tightly or turn the wrist. The lady's fingers should rest lightly over the man's hand, palm to palm. The couple's joined hands are approximately at eye level. The man's left forearm should be inclined slightly forward.

The man stands on his right foot and extends his left leg back, making a longer line. He now invites the lady's right side to his right side by drawing his left elbow backwards; the left hand will now be raised to eye level, with the forearm at 45 degrees. The left elbow should be level with the shoulder.

The lady will now be standing with her right side to the man's right side. Hips should be parallel to each other. The lady must not stand too close to allow for extension and should project forward and up. The lady starts with her right arm in front and keeps this position when the man draws her in; the lady should not move her upper body forward so as to cause the right shoulder and upper arm to move back. Keep the right elbow naturally curved and avoid straightening the arm.

The lady should have her left arm out to the side when walking in to the man and she does not put this down until the man has placed his right wrist in position, when she will rest her left hand on the man's arm by the deltoid muscle just below the top of the shoulder. The muscle should rest between the thumb and forefinger with a slight turn of the wrist moving the four fingers slightly left. The lady should slightly flex the knee of her right foot forward.

The man then places his right wrist just under where the lady's arm meets the back of her shoulder, i.e. armpit. His right hand closes, cupping the shoulder blade with all the fingers closed together, bending the right elbow.

When first learning to dance, it is advisable not to try to have an exaggerated extension for the lady. A common mistake made when beginning to dance is that the lady tries to lean backwards, which is incorrect and can cause many problems. The lady's extension is covered in detail in Chapter 7, under the heading Extension in Lady's Lines, and also in Chapter 3.

So, we can now summarize the five points of body contact when taking hold:

- Man's left hand to lady's right hand.
- Stand off-set to partner – right side to right side.
- Man's right wrist under lady's armpit. Hand cupping lady's shoulder blade.
- Lady's left upper arm on man's forearm.
- Lady's left hand on man's deltoid muscle (side shoulder muscle).

DIRECTION OF DANCE

The first and most important thing to remember is that when dancing around the floor, it is done in an anti-clockwise direction. It is very important to know and understand the direction of the steps around the dance floor, which are referred to as dance alignments.

DANCE ALIGNMENTS

These are the positions of the feet in relation to the room and the direction of travel. Constant referral to these alignments will be made in the dance figures in the following chapters, so you will need to refer to the associated drawing.

- Line of dance
- Against line of dance
- Centre
- Wall
- Diagonal wall
- Diagonal centre

DANCE ALIGNMENTS

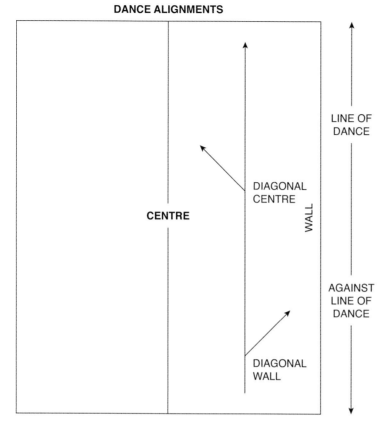

Illustration showing the dance floor indicating the alignments referred
to in the steps.

FOOTWORK

Footwork refers to the action of the foot and it is very important to be precise with the footwork to perform good technique. Sloppy footwork will hinder your dancing and cause a lot of problems, so it is best to work on it and not neglect it.

The feet should not be lifted off the floor, but they should glide along it. An exception to this is the tango footwork, which is explained in Chapter 2 under the heading Tango Footwork. Pay attention to what your feet are doing.

The following footwork applies to the waltz, foxtrot and quickstep only. Tango footwork will be explained as a separate dance, while the Viennese waltz footwork will be explained in Chapter 3.

The term toe is used but includes the use of the ball of the foot as well, while the term heel is used but includes walking on to the whole foot. When the term toe is used on a side step, followed by the closing of one foot to the other, the toe is kept in contact with the floor.

Heel   A heel is the term used when walking forward using the heel of the foot, continuing on to the whole of the foot; the foot is flat – it does not have a rolling action as when doing a heel rising on to a toe.

Heel Toe   A heel toe is the term used when walking forward using the heel of the foot. The weight continues to roll through the foot and then rises up on to the toe of the foot. It would be very difficult to step forward on to a toe from a lowering action, so it will feel normal to do a heel toe.

Toe   A toe is the term used when proceeding forward, sideways or backwards. The step is taken on the ball of the foot and the heel does not touch the floor. The toes only are in contact with the floor; the rest of the foot is off the floor. This footwork is used for maximum rise as in the natural turn in the waltz (step 2).

Toe Heel   A toe heel is the term used when arriving on a toe and continuing to roll through the foot to the heel, in preparation for the next step, as when moving backwards and into the lowering action, and when dancing from a high position to a low position. This action occurs in both the forward and backward actions and allows the ankle to absorb the weight.

Heel Toe Heel   Heel toe heel is the term used when the weight rolls on to the ball of the foot, then

Shows the inside edge of the whole of the foot, which is referred to in the footwork and the steps.

Shows the inside edge of the ball of the foot referred to in the footwork and the steps.

continues to roll into the heel and rolls off the heel at the end. This is used in natural pivoting actions, when dancing from a low position and the step is taken forward from the heel, then the weight moves over to the ball of the foot to allow the foot to pivot and ends with the weight rolling back off of the heel.

Toe Heel Toe   Toe heel toe starts on the toe, the heel is then lowered to the floor very briefly before it is lifted off the floor (sometimes referred to as the heel 'kissing' the floor), ending with pushing off from the toe.

Pointing Toe   Pointing of a toe is when the foot is in a different alignment to the body. The foot is pointing one way and the body is facing another direc-

tion. The foot is pointed in the direction to which you wish to dance.

Inside Edge of Foot   Inside edge of foot is when we are walking using the inside edge of the whole foot or the ball of the foot.

Rise and Fall   This is the elevation and lowering that is produced by the use of the feet, legs and body.

No Foot Rise   This occurs on a backward step when the heel of the supporting foot remains in contact with the floor until the weight is completely transferred. The rise is in the body and legs only, e.g. the lady's feather step in the foxtrot and the man's step in the reverse wave.

TANGO FOOTWORK

Tango footwork is unlike the other four dances. The mechanics of tango are different and, therefore, the technique and footwork will be different. There is no rise and fall. In tango, the foot is slightly lifted and then placed on every step. In the other four dances, the feet have a gliding action into position.

Heel   Heel is a step that is taken on the heel and the foot is then lowered to a flat position; it does not have the smooth rolling action. This is how the basic walk is danced in tango.

Ball Heel   Ball heel starts on the ball of the foot and not the toe, the weight rolls through the foot and rolls off the heel at the end of the step. This is used when walking backwards in tango.

Whole Foot   Whole foot is when the whole of the foot is placed down on to the floor in one action; this footwork is danced in the last step of the closed promenade.

Inside Edge of Foot   Inside edge of foot is when we are walking using the inside edge of the whole foot or ball of the foot.

THE IMPORTANCE OF STRONG ANKLES

The use of the ankle is very important for the dancer and should be strong – weak ankles can result in injury, sprains or even breaks. Neglecting this joint can cause many difficulties in dancing, resulting in poor and incorrect footwork. The movements of the ankle joint are flexion and pointing, inversion and eversion, which allow for the ankle to move in a circular movement. Eversion allows for stabilization when walking or running on uneven surfaces. The rise and fall in ballroom dancing, and the use of the balls of the feet and balancing, all require strong ankles. The heel height of some of the lady's shoes also requires the ankle to work harder to raise the heel off the floor. A common injury is what is known

in sports as a rolled ankle – this is when the ankle inverts too far and injures the joint.

Exercises to strengthen the ankles are in Chapter 9.

EXPLANATIONS OF TERMS USED IN THE BOOK

Closed Position Right Side to Right Side

This is the most basic position we learn when beginning to dance. The man and lady stand right side to right side and are in contact with each other. The hips are parallel to each other.

This position includes outside your partner positions. In outside your partner positions, the hips are the same but the direction of movement is not forward and backwards, but diagonally forward to the left or diagonally backwards to the right. This will allow for the legs to be able to swing through. Outside your partner positions include feather step in the foxtrot, forward lock in the quickstep and outside spin in the waltz.

The closed position is used in most basic figures, e.g. reverse turn in the tango, natural turn in the waltz and Viennese waltz.

Wing Position Left Side to Left Side

The wing position is a difficult figure to learn and achieve while maintaining a good frame and top line. The man and lady are facing each other but the lady is on the man's left side while maintaining the hips parallel. The man's left side and the lady's left side are in contact with each other.

Wing position is used in the closed wing, as well as the wing, and in the hover cross in the foxtrot.

Promenade Position

This is a position where both the man and lady are facing and dancing in the same direction (and not the usual man facing forward, while the lady is dancing backwards). The man's right side and the lady's left side are in contact at ribcage level, leaving the opposite sides of the body open to form a slight 'V'-shape. It is important to point out here that when using the term 'V'-shape, this is a narrow 'V'

Common mistakes that may occur are the right shoulder will go into the lady's space and the right elbow will go behind the body. The elbows must stay up and slightly in front of the body.

Lady

Standing in the closed position, keep shoulders parallel to the man and turn the left hip to sit behind the man's right hip. Make sure the shoulders are still parallel, as much as is possible.

Common Mistakes that May Occur

The lady opens out her body and the shoulders are no longer parallel. The hip has not stayed behind the man's and ends up at the side of the man's hip, or even in front. When trying to keep the shoulders parallel, it is acceptable if they are slightly off parallel.

When turning to the right into the promenade position, at the point of opening the man's feet and hips, do not turn. The shoulders will turn to the right through rotation of the back around the spine. The lady will not turn her shoulders but will turn her hips, knees and feet.

Moving in the promenade position can be difficult to dance correctly; it requires stepping across yourself and keeping the shoulders parallel.

Counter-Promenade Position

Counter-promenade position is another difficult position to dance and can easily disturb the frame and top line if not performed well. Both the man's and lady's hips are open to form a V-shape. The lady's left hip is slightly in front of the man's right hip. If you have mastered the promenade position, when the lady's hip is behind the man's, then dancing the counter-promenade position might be easier to understand and perform if you think of it as the promenade position but with the hips reversed, i.e. the man's hip is behind the lady's; or to see it as promenade going backwards. The man can lead the lady to turn her hips away from him or the man can turn his hips around the lady; this will depend on the figure that is being danced. The counter-promenade includes other figures such as the counter-fallaway position, which is a promenade moving backwards.

Demonstrates a promenade position referred to in the routines, which shows that both partners are facing and travelling in the same direction.

and not a completely open-couple shape, thereby leaving the partnership in a strained position. The lady should try to keep a right side but should turn the hip to be comfortably behind the man's right hip. Even though there is a V-shape, the bodies are still rotated towards each other.

The promenade is a semi-closed position, where both the man and the lady are facing and dancing in the same direction.

Man

Standing in the closed position, keep the shoulders parallel to the lady. Turn the hips to the direction you want to travel in, but continue to keep the shoulders parallel.

Demonstrates outside your partner position from a man's perspective.

Demonstrates outside your partner position from a lady's perspective.

Counter-fallaway is used in the three fallaways in the foxtrot.

Outside your Partner

This is when we step outside our partner on the right, e.g. the man's feather step and the lady's reverse wave, or the chase in tango.

Contrary Body Movement Position (CBMP)

Contrary body movement position is a foot position and not a body action. It is constantly used in steps taken in the promenade position and outside your partner steps in order to maintain the relative body position of the couple. Contrary body movement position is when a foot is placed on or across the line of the standing foot, either in front or behind, to maintain a position, e.g. turning the right side of the body towards a left moving leg; or, conversely, turning the left side of the body towards a right moving leg; the body and leg move at the same time, e.g. step three of the feather step in foxtrot.

Demonstrates a foot position when a foot is placed on or across the line of the standing foot. This is contrary body movement position.

Demonstrates a body action that has been used to initiate turn in the body only, before stepping outside your partner. This is contrary body movement.

Contrary Body Movement (CBM)

Contrary body movement is an action made by the body when turning the opposite side of the body towards the foot that is moving; the direction will be either forward or backwards to start the turn. For example, the man's first step of a feather step contrary body movement is at the end of the first step to initiate the turn; the body turns only, before stepping outside the partner. Another example of CBM is on the first step of the natural turn in the waltz, when the man steps forward on the right foot to commence to turn to the right with Contrary Body Movement. The lady steps backwards on the left foot to commence to turn to the right. A further example of CBM is in the reverse turn, when the man steps forward on the left foot to commence to turn to the left at the end of the step with Contrary Body Move-

ment. The lady steps backwards with the right foot to commence to turn to the left. Although the upper body is turning, the moving foot will sometimes turn out relative to the leg and hip, and sometimes when the toe is turned in.

A forward step with contrary body movement, whether it be the man or lady, is on the outside of the turn and travels more. Although the step is straight on the line that is being danced, the opposite shoulder will be turning towards the moving foot.

CBM AND CBMP

There can be a lot of confusion about CBM and CBMP, and the following explanation may help if you are still not sure.

CBMP

When taking a normal step, the feet will be on two tracks. When in CBMP, the feet will be on one track. Across in CBMP is when the moving leg will go across the standing foot. If stepping in line or across, you have stepped into CBMP. If stepping normally and rotating the body, you have rotated into CBMP. CBMP is used when stepping outside the partner, when your inside foot steps forward in the promenade position or the outside foot steps backwards in a fallaway position. There may be other places, but these are the most common.

CBM

When using CBM, it is only the body that turns and the hips and feet do not, e.g. in a turn to the right at the end of step one in the natural turn for the man, CBM is used.

Summing Up

- CBMP is a position where the body, hips and feet are facing the same direction.
- CBM is a movement where the body only turns, and the feet and hips do not turn.

When taking a backward step in contrary body movement, the dancer would be on the inside of the turn.

Side Leads
This is when taking a step with the same side of the body, either forward or backwards, with the corresponding moving foot, e.g. step with the left foot and left side or the right foot and right side.

Commence to Turn to the Left or to the Right
When the term Contrary Body Movement is used, we are initiating a turn to the left or the right. This is done at the end of a step when there has been a complete change of weight. This is achieved by a slight turn of the ribcage and back. Do not swing a left or right shoulder forward, thereby making the opposite one go backwards and creating energy in the shoulders, but let the shoulders respond in a natural way from the movement in the ribcage and back.

The commence to turn is done at the end of the step and not at the beginning. Turning at the beginning of the step will result in dancing into our partner, causing the partnership to go off-balance.

A more detailed explanation of natural and reverse turns will be covered in Chapter 7.

Brush Step
This is when one foot is brushed to the other foot with no weight. The ball of the foot is in contact with the floor and not the heel, e.g. the lady's spin turn.

Forward Ending to the Side
This is on steps where swinging a leg in a forward direction, but ends in a sideways position. We have turned the hip of the moving leg to end sideways instead of forward, e.g. the man's reverse turn in foxtrot and fallaways.

Natural and Reverse Turns
A natural turn is a turn to the right and a reverse turn is one to the left. This will be explained in more detail in Chapter 7.

Closing of the Feet
When closing one foot to the other from a side position; it closes with the toe in contact with the floor.

Pivots
A pivot is a turn on the ball or the heel of one foot. The amount of turn varies from half or less. There are several different kinds of pivots:

- Toe pivot: turning on the ball of the foot.
- Heel pivot: a turn on the heel.
- Slip pivot: when the foot is slipped through into position without the body moving and then the pivot is executed on the toe.
- Natural and reverse pivots: simply indicate the direction of the turn – natural is to the right and reverse is to the left.

When pivoting, the free leg is held in the contrary body movement position with no weight. It is important that the dancer is balanced over the pivoting foot. The follower always maintains two tracks for the feet on a pivot turn to enable the leader to step between the partner's feet for the next figure. The person stepping forward into the pivot needs to be able to get around their partner without dancing into them. This is where inside and outside of turns need to be mastered.

A pivot on both feet is called a twist turn.

Pivoting Action
When contrary body movement is not held, and disappears quickly, it is called a pivoting action. An example would be the natural spin turn in the waltz, where the lady has a pivoting action and the man pivots on step four (*see* Chapter 3).

Pivots and pivoting action are both explained in more detail in Chapter 7.

Heel Pull
A heel pull is a type of heel turn and will always be to the right. The turn is made on the heel of the standing foot, e.g. step back on the left foot, turn on the left foot, while the right foot is pulled back and to the side of the standing foot, with the feet slightly apart;

it's pulled back first on the heel, then the inside edge of the foot and then flat.

Heel Turn

Heel turns can be made to the left or to the right, e.g. the lady's reverse turn in the foxtrot is a heel turn to the left – a reverse turn.

Start with the weight on the left foot. Step backwards with the right foot, toe lowering the heel. Contrary body position will be at the end of step one. Connect the right side down like an anchor to the right foot. Maintaining the right side to your partner, stretch through the left side with a left side lead. Pull the left foot in to the right foot, dragging the heel with no weight, stretching the centre, but not turning it. When the left foot comes in to the right foot, the turn is made on the right foot using the momentum of the left foot coming in. Keep the knees slightly flexed and soft.

When turning, there is no weight on the closing foot. As the turn is completed, the weight is transferred on to the left foot. After the turn is completed, the weight can be transferred to the balls of both feet, making it more stable to rise up or you can stay on the left foot only, preparing to step forward with the right foot, toe lowering the heel.

GENERAL COMMENTS ON EFFECTIVE PARTNERSHIP

It is often thought that when dancing, the man is the leader and the lady is the follower and that the lady has to dance whatever the man is leading, whether he is dancing it right or wrong; this can be seen as correct but it would be more beneficial to the partnership if the man tried to perfect his dancing to lead more efficiently. When dancing a backward step, the man should not lead by pulling away from his lady because he may feel he is the leader, but he should instead be guided backwards by the lady dancing forward.

Clearly, we can only have one person directing the routine or steps but it is only the job of this person to give a signal as to what is intended to be danced and, therefore, this signal has to be clear and correct.

If the signal is ambiguous, the partner can easily wrong foot the lady by giving her mixed signals. There should be no pulling or pushing the lady into a position or a step. The lady dancer should have her own knowledge of the steps, timing, footwork and alignments, and should not rely on the man to place her somewhere, but should be able to dance herself there. When the man gives the lady a signal as to what he intends to do, the lady should respond and dance her own step confidently to her position; she must learn to react quickly and positively.

It would be beneficial for both parties to work on awareness of movement, body weight and balance to enable them to respond and work together.

The man's right arm is a guide for the lady and his centre is always angled to his right hand. Where the man's right arm goes, so will the lady. Therefore, the man must be correct in the positioning of his hand to his centre. If the centre is turned off, the lady will not go where the man may wish her to go. The lady is in the man's arm and should not be hanging on to it. The lady's centre is also towards the man and not turned under his right arm. Where the man's right arm goes, the lady will be led that way, but she still has to use her feet and legs, and know where she is going, to be able to maintain her position and dance her own steps.

Many times it is said by ladies, 'If only I had a good male dancer, then I would be able to dance.' This is not necessarily true. If the lady is a good dancer and finds a man of equal standard, as a couple, they will be able to perform good dancing. If the lady has just started to dance and chooses to dance with a partner of a high standard, it does not necessarily mean that she will be able to dance to an equally high standard, if she does not have enough knowledge and understanding to be able to follow.

It may help her in her dancing to have a partner of a higher standard but she will still have to learn her own dancing to be able to contribute to the partnership on equal terms. It is not possible for a man to make a lady a better dancer just because he is of a higher standard of dancing.

When starting out with a partner, lead and follow can prove to be difficult and the responsibility should

An effective partnership is the responsibility of both the leader and the follower.

not just be left to the man, with the lady saying 'but you did not lead me'. It would be beneficial for the lady to have enough knowledge to be able to help the man with this difficult task by being aware of her own timing, steps, footwork, directions, and what is required in leading and following. Being aware of what the man is trying to convey, and how he should convey it, are essential to the dance partnership. If the lady also learns to dance the role of the man, then this can be productive and helpful. Also, it will prove most useful for the man to have knowledge of the lady's role in dancing and her steps.

In the next paragraphs we are covering the forward and backward actions. It might be helpful to point out now, that when the lady is stepping forward, it would be beneficial for the man to monitor her lowering so as not to pull the lady off of her feet. The man should not just power away regardless of his partner's capability to lower. It is important at all stages of your dancing to think about awareness again, as mentioned above, of the partner's movement, hold and posture, and be aware of any difficulties that are being experienced or felt. It is only by knowledge and working out problems together that the answer can be found. Statements such as: 'You should follow' and 'You should lead', will prove to be very unproductive.

If you are starting out with a partner, you should bear this in mind. It may prevent a lot of disagreements, and will also be helpful to improving the partnership, if both parties are knowledgeable of their own dancing. Many of the man's steps are the lady's steps in reverse, e.g. the reverse wave in the foxtrot.

If you are starting out without a partner, your dancing can be improved by practising alone. Learn all the techniques, timing, footwork and positions, and be capable of dancing them alone without the music and then with the music.

THE PREPARATION STEP EXPLAINED

A question that is always asked is, 'How do I know which foot the man is going to start on?' A preparation step is a step that prepares the dancer to start

dancing – it initiates movement, it is not a figure and it is not compulsory to start the dance with. Why it is done is to help the lady to know where the balance of the partnership is and to make sure that she feels where the weight of the man is, so as to start on the correct foot. Preparation to move can be very subtle or very elaborate; it would depend on our level of dancing.

As a beginner, it would be advisable to prepare to dance from just one step as a preparation, instead of the more elaborate one that requires three steps.

The beginner may want to just take one step forward as a preparation step; this would be preceding the figure to be danced. For example, in the natural turn in the waltz, the man should stand on his right foot with a nice soft, slightly flexed knee and his weight settled completely on the right foot. Step forward with the left foot with the body slightly turned to the left on the beat of three in the music, ready to proceed with step one of the natural turn.

The same would apply to the foxtrot, starting with a feather step, but the man would be stepping forward on the beat of four in the music with his left foot. For the quickstep, starting with the natural turn, the man would step forward on the left foot on the beat of eight in the music.

It is best to leave a more elaborate preparation for the advanced dancer.

In the following chapters, the book will cover a basic and an improver's routine for each of the five dances:

- The English or standard waltz and the Viennese waltz.
- The slow foxtrot.
- The quickstep.
- The ballroom tango.

Learning to dance these routines involves mastering the three following phases:

1. Learning the routines solo, whether as man or lady, without the music.
2. Learning to dance these routines with a partner without the music.

3. Learning to dance these routines with a partner and with the music.

Learning the choreography slowly and at your own pace, paying careful attention to the room and the dance alignments, will be of help.

In the following chapters of the book we will cover the beginner and improver's steps of the five ballroom dances. We have deliberatively kept the routines simple, so as to enable the novice dancer to concentrate on achieving the correct technique of movement to accomplish the basic choreography. The aim is to dance on balance and in control, to achieve beautiful dancing and not to dance too advanced a choreography ahead of our ability to perform good technique, which often results in untidy, unbalanced, incorrect dancing. The reader should aim to perfect these essentials to ultimately enjoy their dancing. The many problems that may occur when learning to dance without these basic essentials can lead to a breakdown of the partnership. A memory of incorrect dancing can take a very long time to correct and, ultimately, lead to a dream shattered that could have been achieved. Trying to learn very advanced choreography may seem exciting but without good understanding and ability it can prove to be very difficult and unsightly.

Having got this far, and having studied the ideas we have elucidated above, we are ready to begin dancing!

You will soon discover that when trying to dance in the way the instructions are given will at first not appear to feel comfortable or indeed natural. This is perfectly normal. You might have watched professional dancers and get a feeling that what you are dancing in no way resembles the look you have seen. This is also perfectly normal. You might feel that there is some magical secret that these dancers possess that enables them to dance as they do. The fact is that there is no magical secret other than to follow and practise the fundamentals of dancing expounded in this book. A very wise commentator of ballroom dancing once described the wonderful dancing of the World Professional Ballroom Champion as being achieved through 5 per cent inspiration and 95 per cent perspiration. The three words to achieving perfection of dance must be: practice, practice and practice!

You will feel at the beginning that even standing correctly, your stance feels wrong. This, again, is perfectly natural, as you will be using unfamiliar muscles to attain the desired posture.

When you start to move, it will feel awkward, as most people need to relearn how to walk correctly before they can dance well. Dancing, in reality, is only an extension of walking correctly. We have been walking almost from our first birthday but have we been walking correctly? Babies will emulate the movements of their parents. You only have to watch a group of people moving down the street to see this; they will all have different gaits. A well-known fitness expert stated that walking correctly is not instinctive. Walking correctly uses all the muscles of your legs and feet, not just a few. In addition, it will necessitate the correct usage of the muscles in your back and chest to maintain your posture. Bad posture in walking can be seen in people hunching or slouching. Finally, it is necessary to learn how to use the feet correctly when walking. This involves rolling the weight correctly from the heel to the ball of the foot and forward on to all of the toes. We need to perform all of these actions before striking the next heel. Even this apparently simple action requires practice and more practice to perfect.

CHAPTER 3

THE WALTZ – ENGLISH AND VIENNESE

The English waltz, often called the slow waltz or international waltz, is perhaps the oldest of all the classical ballroom dances. It is deeply rooted in both culture and tradition, and was born out of the European or Viennese waltz, the latter being originally an Austrian folk dance. The word 'waltz' originates from the Latin word 'volvere' meaning 'to roll'. The German word 'waltzer' also means to roll or to turn.

In its original form, the waltz was danced in a rotary fashion, with the man dancing a forward step with the right foot, left foot to the side and in front, and across the path of his lady, and then closing right foot to left. He would then repeat these three steps in a backward direction. This would give the partnership six steps in a rotating motion, turning all the time, which would continue all around the room. As time went on, a 'change step' was introduced after the first six steps (now called the natural turn), which allowed the next six steps to be danced turning to the left (called the reverse turn). The tempo was also slowed down so that the dance was danced much more slowly. Progressive steps were introduced so that the dance could move along what is now called the line of dance.

1921 was the year when the waltz came into its own as a result of a great conference

Beginner's routine waltz.

held in England. The closed hold was standardized together with the establishment of left and right turns. The waltz is regarded by many people as the most romantic of all the ballroom dances because of the feel of the music and the relative easy flow of the dance. It is characterized by its pendulum swinging action coupled with its graceful rise and fall, and an easy rotary action.

The English waltz, unlike the American waltz, is danced in what we call a closed hold. It is danced in 3/4 time with a strong accentuation on the first beat of the bar of the music. One step is taken for each beat of music. So the timing of the steps would be one, two, three to each bar of music.

As we advance and get better, and begin to feel the music, this timing will change to one, twooooo, three, as we 'steal' a bit of time from the third beat. This is called 'rubato' from the Italian word meaning 'to rob' in between the beats. We will discuss more about this in Chapter 8 under the heading Dancing Musically.

More advanced steps might have four, five or six steps for a bar of music.

THE ENGLISH WALTZ – BASIC BEGINNER'S ROUTINE

The Natural Turn
The timing of this figure is: one two three – four five six.

Man   Rise and fall – commence to rise at the end of step one, continue to rise on steps two and three, lowering the heel at the end of step three.

Commence to rise at the end of step four, no foot rise, continue to rise on steps five and six, lowering the heel at the end of step six.

Lady   Rise and fall – commence to rise at the end of step one, no foot rise, continue to rise on steps two and three, lowering the heel at the end of step three.

Commence to rise at the end of step four, continue to rise on steps five and six, lowering the heel at the end of step six.

Step One
Man   Facing the diagonal wall, step forward with the right foot on the heel, rising up on to the toe, commencing to turn to the right.

Lady   Lady backing the diagonal wall, step backwards, on the left foot on the toe, lowering the heel, no foot rise, commencing to turn right.

Step Two
Man   Step forward ending to the side on the left foot on a toe, to end backing the diagonal centre.

Lady   Step to the side on the right foot on the toe, pointing the toe down the line of dance.

Step Three
Man   Close the right foot to the left foot on the toe, lowering the heel to end backing the line of dance.

Lady   Close the left foot to the right foot on a toe, lowering the heel, to end facing the line of dance.

Step one of a natural turn in the waltz.

Step two of a natural turn in the waltz.

Step three of a natural turn in the waltz.

The photograph End of Step Three shows the collection preparing for the following step.

Step Four
Man   Backing the line of dance, step backwards on the left foot on the toe, lowering the heel, no foot rise, commencing to turn to the right.

Lady   Facing the line of dance, step forward with the right foot on the heel, rising up on to the toe, commencing to turn right.

Step Five
Man   Step to the side on the right foot on a toe, with the toe pointing to the diagonal centre.

Lady   Step to the side on the left foot, backing centre on a toe.

Step Six
Man   Close the left foot to the right foot to end facing the diagonal centre on the toe, lowering the heel.

End of step three of a natural turn showing the collection of weight before commencing step four.

Step four of a natural turn in the waltz.

Step five of a natural turn in the waltz.

Lady Close the right foot to the left foot, on a toe, lowering the heel, to end backing the diagonal centre.

Change Step Natural to Reverse

The timing of this figure is: one two three.

Man Rise and fall – commence to rise at the end of step one, continue to rise on steps two and three, lowering the heel at the end of step three.

Lady Rise and fall – commence to rise at the end of step one with no foot rise, continue to rise on steps two and three, lowering the heel at the end of step three.

Step One
Man Facing the diagonal centre, step forward on the right foot on the heel, rising up on to the toe.

Lady Backing the diagonal centre, step backwards on the left foot on the toe, lowering the heel with no foot rise.

Step six of a natural turn in the waltz.

Step one of a change step natural to reverse in the waltz.

Step two of a change step natural to reverse in the waltz.

Step three of a change step natural to reverse in the waltz.

End of step three of a change step natural to reverse showing the collection of weight before commencing the following step.

Step Two

Man   Facing the diagonal centre, step to the side and slightly forward on the left foot on a toe.

Lady   Backing the diagonal centre, step to the side and slightly back on the right foot on the toe.

Step Three

Man   Facing the diagonal centre, close the right foot to the left foot on the toe, lowering the heel.

Lady   Backing the diagonal centre, close the left foot to the right foot on the toe, lowering the heel.
   The photograph End of Step Three is collection preparing for the following step.

Reverse Turn

The timing of this figure is: one two three four five six.

Man   Rise and fall – commence to rise at the end of step one, continue to rise on steps two and three, lowering the heel at the end of step three. Commence to rise at the end of step four with no foot rise, continue to rise on steps five and six, lowering the heel at the end of step six.

Lady   Rise and fall – commence to rise at the end of step one with no foot rise, continue to rise on steps two and three, lowering the heel at the end of step three. Commence to rise at the end of step four, continue to rise on steps five and six, lowering the heel at the end of step six.

Step One

Man   Facing the diagonal centre, step forward on the left foot on the heel, rising up on to the toe commencing to turn to the left.

Lady   Backing the diagonal centre, step backwards on the right foot with no foot rise, on the toe lowering the heel, commencing to turn to the left.

Step Two

Man   Step forward and slightly to the side on the right foot on the toe, to end backing the diagonal wall.

Lady   Step to the side on the left foot on the toe, pointing the toe down the line of dance.

Step Three

Man   Close the left foot to the right foot on the toe, lowering the heel to end backing the line of dance.

Lady   Close the right foot to the left foot on the toe, lowering the heel to end facing the line of dance.

Step one of a reverse turn in the waltz.

Step two of a reverse turn in the waltz.

Step three of a reverse turn in the waltz.

Step Four

Man   Backing the line of dance, step backwards on the right foot, on the toe, lowering the heel with no foot rise, commencing to turn to the left.

Lady   Facing the line of dance, step forward on the left foot on the heel, rising up on to the toe commencing to turn to the left.

Step Five

Man   Step to the side on the left foot, pointing the toe to the diagonal wall on the toe.

Lady   Step forward and slightly to the side on the right foot on the toe, to end backing the wall.

Step Six

Man   Close the right foot to the left foot on the toe, lowering the heel, to end facing the diagonal wall.

Lady   Close the left foot to the right foot on the toe, lowering the heel to end backing the diagonal wall.

Step four of a reverse turn in the waltz.

Step five of a reverse turn in the waltz.

Step six of a reverse turn in the waltz.

Change Step – Reverse to Natural

The timing of this figure is: one two three.

Man   Rise and fall – commence to rise at the end of step one, continue to rise on steps two and three, lowering the heel at the end of step three.

Lady   Rise and fall – commence to rise at the end of step one with no foot rise, continue to rise on steps two and three, lowering the heel at the end of step three.

Step One
Man   Facing the diagonal wall, step forward on the left foot on a heel rising up on to the toe.

Lady   Backing the diagonal wall, step backwards on the right foot on the toe, lowering the heel with no foot rise.

Step one of a change step reverse to natural in the waltz.

Step two of a change step reverse to natural in the waltz.

Step three of a change step reverse to natural in the waltz.

Step Two
Man Step forward and slightly to the side on the right foot on the toe.

Lady Step backwards and slightly to the side on the left foot on the toe.

Step Three
Man Close the left foot to the right foot on the toe, lowering the heel to end facing the diagonal wall.

Lady Close the right foot to the left foot on the toe, lowering the heel to end backing the diagonal wall.

These are the basic eighteen steps for beginner dancers and this routine can be repeated continuously around the dance floor. The improver's steps can be danced once the beginner dancer has reached a standard of comfortably dancing this basic routine.

THE IMPROVER'S STEPS

Natural Spin Turn
Having danced the first three steps of the natural turn, continue with the following steps for the spin turn.
The timing of this figure is: four five six.

Man Rise and fall – rise at the end of step five up and lower at the end of step six.

Lady Rise and fall – rise at the end of step five up and lower at the end of step six.

Step Four
Man Backing the line of dance, step backwards on the left foot, turning the toe inwards and dancing toe, heel, toe; this is a pivot to the right lowering the heel and keeping the heel in contact with the floor while turning to end facing the line of dance.

Lady Facing the line of dance, step forward on the right foot on the heel, rising up on to the ball of the foot, turning to the right, using a pivoting action to end backing the line of dance.

Step Five
Man Facing the line of dance, step forward on the right foot in the contrary body movement position on the heel rising up on to the toe.

Lady Backing the line of dance, step backwards and slightly to the side on the left foot on the toe, continuing to turn to face the diagonal centre.

Step Six
Man Step to the side and slightly back on the left foot on the toe, lowering the heel, continuing to turn ending backing the diagonal centre.

Lady Brush right foot to left foot before stepping out diagonally on the right foot, on the toe, lowering the heel. This is called a Brush Step and has also been explained in Chapter 2.
Continue to dance steps four five six of a reverse turn, followed by a whisk.

Step four of a natural spin turn in the waltz.

Step five of a natural spin turn in the waltz.

Step six of a natural spin turn in the waltz.

Whisk

The timing of this figure is: one two three.

Man Rise and fall – commence to rise at the end of step one, continue to rise on step two, continuing to rise and lowering at the end of step three.

Lady Rise and fall – commence to rise at the end of step one, no foot rise, continue to rise on step two, up and lower at the end of step three.

Step One
Man Facing the diagonal wall, step forward on the left foot on the heel, rising up on to the toe.

Lady Backing the diagonal wall, step backwards on the right foot on the toe, lowering the heel. No foot rise.

Step Two
Man Step to the side and slightly forward on the right foot on the toe, facing the diagonal wall.

Lady Step diagonally back on the left foot on a toe, pointing the toe to the diagonal centre.

Step Three
Man Left foot crosses behind the right foot in the promenade position on the toe, lowering the heel, to end facing the diagonal wall.

Lady Right foot crosses behind the left foot in the promenade position on the toe, lowering the heel to end facing diagonal centre.

Chasse from Promenade

The timing of this figure is: one and two three.

Man   Rise and fall – commence to rise at the end of step one, continue to rise on steps two and three, up and lower at the end of step four.

Lady   Rise and fall – commence to rise at the end of step one, continue to rise on steps two and three, up and lower at the end of step four.

Step One
Man   Facing the diagonal wall, step forward and across with the right foot in the promenade position and in the contrary body movement position on the heel, rising up on to the toe, moving along the line of dance.

Lady   Facing the diagonal centre, step forward and across on the left foot in the promenade position and in the contrary body movement position on the heel, rising up on to the toe, moving along the line of dance, commencing to turn to the left.

Step Two
Man   Step to the side and slightly forward on the left foot on the toe, facing the diagonal wall.

Lady   Step to the side, on the right foot on the toe, to end backing wall.

Step Three
Man   Close the right foot to the left foot on the toe, facing the diagonal wall.

Lady   Close the left foot to the right foot on the toe, backing the diagonal wall.

Step Four
Man   Facing the diagonal wall, step to the side and slightly forward on the left foot on the toe, lowering the heel.

Lady   Backing the diagonal wall, step to the side and slightly backwards on the right foot on the toe, lowering the heel.
   When reaching a corner dance a natural spin turn,

commencing with steps one two and three of the natural turn. Continue with steps one, two and three of the spin turn.

Turning Lock Opening to Promenade
The timing of this figure is: one and two three.

Man   Rise and fall – commence to rise at the end of step one, continue to rise on steps two and three, up and lower at the end of step four.

Lady   Rise and fall – commence to rise at the end of step one, continue to rise on steps two and three, up and lower at the end of step four.

Step One
Man   Backing the line of dance, step backwards on the right foot with the right side leading on the toe.

Lady   Facing the line of dance, step forward on the left foot with the left side leading on the toe.

Step Two
Man   Left foot crosses in front of the right foot, facing the centre, on the toe.

Lady   Cross the right foot behind the left foot, backing the centre, on the toe.

Step Three
Man   Step forward and slightly to the side with a small step on the toe, in between the partner's feet, on the right foot facing the diagonal centre.

Lady   Step to the side and slightly back with the left foot, backing the diagonal centre on the toe.

Step Four
Man   Step forward and slightly to the side on the left foot, with the left side leading, in the promenade position, pointing the toe to the diagonal centre, with the body facing the line of dance on the toe, lowering the heel. There is a slight body turn to the right.

Lady   Step to the side on the right foot on the toe, lowering the heel in the promenade position, having brushed towards the left foot, pointing the toe to the centre and moving to the diagonal centre.

Continue with a progressive chasse dancing diagonal to the centre following with steps one, two and three of the change step – natural to reverse.

DOUBLE REVERSE SPIN

The timing of this figure is: one two and three.

Improver's timing can be: one two three and.

Man   Rise and fall – rise at the end of step one, up on step two, up and lower at the end of step three.

Lady   Rise and fall – rise slightly at the end of step one, no foot rise, continue to rise on step two, up on step three, up and lower at the end of step four.

The double reverse spin can be danced commencing with the diagonal centre, diagonal wall or line of dance.

Step One
Man   Facing the diagonal centre, step forward on the left foot, commencing to turn left on the heel, rising up on to the toe.

Lady   Backing the diagonal centre, step backwards on the right foot on the toe, lowering the heel, commencing to turn to the left.

Step Two
Man   Step forward and to the side on the right foot to end backing the diagonal wall on the toe.

Lady   Close the left foot to the right foot (this is a heel turn; *see* Chapter 2) to end facing the line of dance. The heel of the left foot skims the floor, turn on the right foot rising up on to the toe of the right foot.

Step Three
Man   Close the left foot to the right foot, without

weight, on the toe. Pivot on the right foot, to end facing the diagonal wall on a toe, lowering the heel of the right foot.

Lady   Step to the side and slightly back on the right foot, on a toe, to end backing wall.

Step Four
Lady Only   Cross the left foot in front of the right foot on the toe, lowering the heel to end backing the diagonal wall.

The routine can start again with the change step, natural turn and spin turn.

THE DOUBLE REVERSE SPIN EXPLAINED IN DETAIL

The double reverse spin can be a difficult step to perform, so here we explain it in more detail to help overcome some of the problems that may occur. A lot of problems occur when rotation is put in too early. Imagine a picture of two dancers moving but not together, but with a movement of 'you go, I go'. On step one, the man steps forward and should step straight, he should not start turning to the left at the beginning of his step as this will create a problem for the lady by turning her in front of him, which will make the step very difficult. Step one for both man and lady is straight and moves down the line of dance. At the end of step one, with the weight fully on the foot, the man starts his turn to the left with his body, contrary body movement. On step two, the man continues to go forward but ends to the side; this allows for the man to move past the lady. At this point, the lady is doing a heel turn and she is the centre of the turn, which she holds as the man is moving past her. Once the man has arrived on his toe for his toe pivot, he is now the centre of the turn and the lady moves around the man. This will be step three for the lady and she must make sure that she turns her hip back to close to the man. The partner that is holding the centre of the turn is not travelling and must be seen as an anchor to allow the other partner to move past freely.

The Viennese waltz.

This step is not danced with both partners moving and rotating at the same time. It is danced in two rotational parts. The end of step two for the man is a toe pivot, which is rotational – the man is rotating around the lady. The end of step one and the beginning of step two is the heel turn for the lady. The man anchors at the end of step two, while the lady moves past the man and turns back to the man on step three, and crosses in front on step four. This is also rotational as the lady rotates back to the man.

So the 'you go, I go' is very important to learn and master in order to be able to perform the double reverse spin with style, grace and balance.

ENGLISH WALTZ MUSIC SUGGESTIONS

- *Fascination* by Nat King Cole.
- *Could I Have this Dance* by Anne Murray.
- *Nocturne* by Secret Garden.
- *Come Away with Me* by Nora Jones.
- *When Winter Comes* by Chris de Burgh.
- *Moon River* by Andy Williams.
- *My Cup Runneth Over* by Des O'Connor.
- *The Godfather Waltz* by Henry Mancini Orchestra.
- Theme from *Papillon* by Manuel and the Music of the Mountains.
- *You Light Up My Life* by Whitney Houston.

THE VIENNESE WALTZ

The Viennese waltz conjures up images of grand society balls with elegant ladies in fine ball-gowns twirling around with handsome military partners. Today the popularity of the Viennese waltz has been revived by live performances and television broadcasts of the Dutch violinist and conductor Andre Rieu, who with his Johann Strauss Orchestra has achieved almost rock star status.

The Viennese Waltz is ballroom dancing's oldest dance form and pre-dates all the other four dances. It first arose in the late 18th century in the Bavarian region of Austria, although an earlier record indicates a peasant dance being danced in the Provence region of France in the 1560s. Danced in

3/4 time to folk music called the Volta, a word that means 'to turn', it was the first dance to be danced in a close hold. The man held the lady around the waist and the lady placed her right arm on the man's left shoulder. She would hold her gown up off of the floor with her left hand. It has been suggested that the man held the lady in this way to avoid his sword that was held in a scabbard down his left side.

This closed hold, seen as an embrace, was considered very scandalous and immoral, and was banned from the court of Louis XIII. However, the dance become hugely popular in Vienna (giving rise to its name) and large crowds of dancers converged in dance halls and the Sum Speri (built in 1807) and the Apollo (built in 1808).

Perhaps the most famous of the Viennese waltz composers were the father and son, having the same name, Johann Strauss. The son is often referred to as the 'waltz king'.

Like the English waltz, the Viennese waltz is danced in 3/4 time, and has a tempo of between 56 and 60 bars per minute.

THE VIENNESE WALTZ ROUTINE

Rise and Fall   In the Viennese waltz, the rise and fall is felt mainly through the knees and not the feet. When rise is stated, this will mean a very small rise and not a high one as in the English waltz, so the foot rise is kept to a minimum. The Viennese waltz is a relatively flat dance and does not have the deep pendulum swing as in the English waltz.

Natural Turn

Man   Rise and fall – start to rise between steps one and two, and complete the rise between steps two and three. Slight lowering between steps three and four. Start to rise between steps four and five, and complete the rise between steps five and six.

Lady   Rise and fall – start to rise between steps one and two, and complete the rise between steps two and three. Slight lowering between steps three and four. Rise between steps four and five, and complete the rise between steps five and six.

Viennese waltz routine.

Natural Turn

Step One

Man Facing the diagonal centre, step forward with the right foot on a heel toe and end facing the line of dance.

Lady Backing the diagonal centre, step backwards on the left foot, slightly diagonal on a toe, lowering the heel, to end backing the line of dance.

Step Two

Man Step to the side with the left foot on a toe, to end backing centre.

Lady Step to the side with the right foot on a toe, pointing the toe to the diagonal centre.

Step Three

Man Close the right foot to the left foot on a toe, lowering the heel to end backing the diagonal centre.

Lady Close the left foot to the right foot on a toe flat, to end facing the diagonal centre.

Step Four

Man Step backwards slightly diagonal on the left foot, toe flat, to end backing the line of dance.

Lady Step forwards with the right foot heel toe, to end facing the line of dance.

Step Five

Man Step to the side with the right foot on a toe, pointing the toe to the diagonal centre.

Lady Step to the side on the left foot on a toe, to end backing centre.

Step Six

Man Close the left foot to the right foot on a flat foot, to end facing the diagonal centre.

Lady Close the right foot to the left foot on a toe, lowering the heel, to end backing the diagonal centre.

Amount of Turn

Man Commence to turn to the right on step one, a quarter of a turn between steps one and two, one-eighth of a turn between steps two and three, one-eighth of a turn between steps three and four, three-eighths of a turn between steps four and five (the body turns less), and the body completes the turn between steps five and six. The body turns less between steps four and five because the hip is creating the turn. If the body is turned the same amount, the step will be overturned.

Lady Commence to turn to the right on step one, three-eighths between one and two (as above, the body turns less). The body completes the turn between steps two and three, one-eighth between three and four, a quarter between four and five, one-eighth between five and six.

The natural turns are normally danced in bars of eight and then change to reverse turns.

Forward Change Step Natural to Reverse

Rise and Fall Commence to rise at the end of step one and continue to rise between steps one and two, up and lower at the end of step three.

Step One

Man or Lady Commence with facing the diagonal centre. Step forward with the right foot heel toe, to end facing the line of dance.

Step Two

Man or Lady Step forward with the left foot, on a toe, with the left shoulder leading. Left shoulder leading means that the left shoulder is in front of the right shoulder; therefore it leads towards the direction you are moving to.

Step Three

Man or Lady Close the right foot to the left foot, toe lowering the heel, to end facing the line of dance.

Amount of Turn

Man or Lady One-eighth of a turn to the right on

step one, body turns on step two, position held on step three.

Forward Change Step Reverse to Natural
Rise and Fall Commence to rise at the end of step one, continue to rise between steps one and two, up and lower the end of step three.

Step One
Man or Lady Commence with facing the line of dance. Step forward with the left foot heel toe.

Step Two
Man or Lady Step diagonally forward with the right foot on a toe facing the diagonal centre, moving along the line of dance.

Step Three
Man or Lady Close the left foot to the right foot, toe heel, to end facing the diagonal centre.

Amount of Turn
Man or Lady One-eighth of a turn to the left between steps one and two, position held on step two, position held on step three. The position is held, as there is not a turn to another direction, just a slight turn of the shoulders.

Backward Change Step Natural to Reverse
Rise and Fall Commence to rise at the end of step one, no foot rise, continue to rise between steps one and two, up and lower at the end of step three.

Step One
Man or Lady Commence with backing the line of dance. Step backwards on the left foot, toe heel, to end backing the line of dance.

Step Two
Man or Lady Step backwards on the right foot with a right shoulder lead, on a toe backing the line of dance.

Step Three
Man or Lady Close the left foot to the right foot, toe heel backing the line of dance.

Amount of Turn
Man or Lady Commence to turn one-eighth on step one, body turns on step two, position held on step three.

Backward Change Step Reverse to Natural
Rise and Fall Commence to rise at the end of step one, no foot rise, continue to rise between steps one and two, up and lower the end of step three.

Step One
Man or Lady Commence with backing the line of dance. Step backwards on the right foot, toe heel.

Step Two
Man or Lady Step diagonally backwards with the left foot, on a toe backing the diagonal centre and moving along the line of dance.

Step Three
Man or Lady Close the right foot to the left foot, on a toe then lowering the heel, to end backing the diagonal centre.

Amount of Turn
Man or Lady One-eighth of a turn to the left between steps one and two, position held on step two, position held on step three.

Reverse Turn
Rise and Fall Commence to rise between steps one and two. Complete the rise between steps two and three. Start to lower between steps three and four. Complete lowering and start to rise between steps four and five. Complete the rise between steps five and six.

Step One
Man Commence with facing the line of dance, or almost. Step forward with the left foot, heel toe to end facing the line of dance.

Lady Commence with backing the line of dance, or almost. Step backwards and slightly to the side with the right foot, with toe turned in, toe heel.

Step Two

Man Step to the side and slightly backwards, with the right foot, on a toe, to end backing wall.

Lady Step to the side with the left foot pointing foot between the diagonal wall and the line of dance, on a toe.

Step Three

Man Cross the left foot in front of the right foot, toe heel backing the line of dance.

Lady Close the right foot to the left foot almost facing the line of dance, toe heel, flat foot.

Step Four

Man Step backwards and slightly to the side with the right foot with the toe turned in, toe flat backing the line of dance.

Lady Step forward with the left foot heel toe, facing the line of dance.

Step Five

Man Step to the side with the left foot pointing the toe between the diagonal wall and the line of dance, on a toe.

Lady Step to the side and slightly backwards, on the right foot, on a toe, to end backing wall.

Step Six

Man Close the right foot to the left foot on a flat foot, almost facing the line of dance.

Lady Cross the left foot in front of the right foot, toe heel, almost backing the line of dance.

Amount of Turn

Man Commence to turn to the left on step one, a quarter of a turn between steps one and two, a quarter of a turn between steps two and three, one-eighth of a turn between steps three and four, three-eighths of a turn between steps four and five with

the body turning less. The body completes the turn between steps five and six.

Lady Commence to turn left on step one, three-eighths of a turn between steps one and two, body completes turn between steps two and three, slight turn on steps three and four, a quarter of a turn between steps four and five, a quarter of a turn between steps five and six.

When dancing the Viennese waltz, it is correct to dance 16 bars of music before the change to reverse turn or back to natural turn.

In the Viennese waltz, we want to move effortlessly and easily, and trying to turn will prevent the natural flow of the dance. In the natural turn, the person moving forward is the one initiating the movement and will swing past in a forward direction that will end up to the side. Try again to think of 'you go, I go'. The person going forward by just overtaking the partner will make the turn.

The person going backwards is guided by the forward motion of the person going forward. Trying to dance yourself backwards results in loss of posture and is no longer effortless.

VIENNESE WALTZ MUSIC SUGGESTIONS

- *The Blue Danube* by the Joe Loss Orchestra.
- *Roses from the South* by the Willy Ulrich Orchestra.
- *Falling In Love with Love* by the Geoff Love Orchestra.
- *Ballsirenen* by Bela Sanders.
- *Under Paris Skies* by Joe Fingers Carr.
- *That's Amore* by Dean Martin.
- *After the Ball is Over* by Nat King Cole.
- *Que Sera Sera* by Doris Day.
- *Delilah* by Tom Jones.
- *Piano Man* by Billy Joel.
- *Caribbean Blue* by Enya.
- *Kiss from a Rose* by Seal.

CHAPTER 4

THE SLOW FOXTROT

Because of the smoothness and elegance of the slow foxtrot, it is regarded by many people as the 'dancer's dance'. It has evolved today into a dance that captures effortlessness and grace, so much so that it is regarded as the 'Rolls Royce' of all the ballroom dances.

The origin of the foxtrot is generally attributed to the vaudeville actor, Harry Fox. Fox had a career as a baseball player before being hired by the vaudeville theatres, which eventually took him to New York. It was here that, as part of his act on the roof of the theatre 'Jardin de Danse' in the 1920s, he is reputed to have invented a dance consisting of a series of trotting steps to ragtime music, which he called 'Fox's trots'.

However, it was Oscar Duryea, an American dance teacher, who was hired by the American Society of Professors of Dancing to promote this new 'Fox trot', which they had started to standardize; he modified the exhausting Fox's trotting dance to a smoother gliding dance. This 'new foxtrot' was an instant success.

The husband and wife team of Vernon and Irene Castle, as dance teachers, took Fox's dance and refined and remodelled it further using the previously existing one-step, two-step and turkey trot. Thus a new dance was born and was considered a unique and exciting dance. When the competitive dance couple, Anderson and Bradley, brought the foxtrot to England and won several competitions, the dance world was won over by this new dance.

The foxtrot further developed to incorporate the slow syncopation rhythm of the 4/4 time signature, enabling couples to 'move on the spot' on the crowded dance floors of the 1930s and 1940s when the big bands of that era were popularizing 'swing' music.

It is, today, possibly the most popular of all the ballroom dances from a social point of view, but it is often seen as the most difficult of the ballroom dances to learn and to dance because of its combination of slow and quick timings of the steps and the use of heels and toes.

Today's slow foxtrot is characterized by the passing of the feet with long, continuous steps, with the feet, generally, not closing in this dance (however, there are exceptions to this).

THE BEGINNER'S ROUTINE
Feather Step Danced Diagonal Centre
The timing of this figure is: slow quick quick.

The feather step can be danced down the line of dance, diagonal wall or diagonal centre.

The toe of the front foot should be released from the floor as it moves backwards to the standing foot. This enables the heel to skim the floor. Where the instructions state 'no foot rise' but 'up', this means only the body stretches up. The stretch is in the body and legs, not the foot rising up on to a toe.

It is important to understand that in the foxtrot, on every slow step, we are taking up two beats of the bar of music. This can cause a lot of confusion, because we only have three steps in four beats of music and it is tempting to dance four steps.

In the basic routine, you will only be dancing three steps to every bar of music: slow quick quick.

Man Rise and fall – rise at the end of step one, up on step two, up and lower on step three.

The slow foxtrot.

Lady Rise and fall – rise at the end of step one with no foot rise, up on step two no foot rise, up on step three no foot rise, lowering at the end of step three.

Step One

Man Facing the diagonal centre, step forward with the right foot on the heel rising up on to the toe.

Man Backing the diagonal centre, step backwards with the left foot on the toe, lowering the heel, rising up through the body and legs only, as there is no foot rise releasing the toe of the front foot from the floor.

Step Two

Man Step forward, preparing to step outside your partner with the left foot and with the left side leading, on the toe.

Man Step backwards with the right foot, with the right side leading on the toe, lowering the heel, continuing to rise up through the body and legs, releasing the toe of the front foot from the floor.

Step Three

Man Step forward with the right foot in the contrary body movement position, outside your partner, on the toe, lowering the heel.

Man Step backwards with the left foot in the contrary body movement position, on the toe, lowering the heel, continuing to rise up through the body and legs, releasing the toe of the front foot from the floor.

Step one feather step slow foxtrot.

Step two feather step slow foxtrot.

Step three feather step slow foxtrot.

Reverse Turn
The timing of this figure is: slow quick quick.

Man   Rise and fall – rise at the end of step one, up on step two, up and lower at the end of step three.

Lady   Rise and fall – rise slightly at the end of step one with no foot rise, continue to rise on step two, up and lower at the end of step three.

Step One
Man   Facing the diagonal centre, step forward with the left foot on the heel, rising up on to the toe, commencing to turn left.

Lady   Backing the diagonal centre, step back-wards with the right foot on the toe, lowering the heel, rising up through the body only, as there is no foot rise, and releasing the toe of the front foot from the floor, commencing to turn left.

Step Two
Man   Step forward and to the side with the right foot on the toe, to end backing the diagonal wall.

Lady   Close the left foot to the right foot (this is a heel turn), turning on the right foot, keeping the whole of the foot on the floor, slightly flexing the knee, to end facing the line of dance, rising up on to the toes and changing weight to the left foot.
The lady has her feet closed as this is her heel turn, while the man will be with his feet open as he is moving past the lady. (*See* photograph for step two.)

Step Three
Man   Step backwards with the left foot on the toe, lowering the heel, to end backing the line of dance.

Lady   Step forward with the right foot on the toe, lowering the heel, to end facing the line of dance

Step one reverse turn slow foxtrot.

Step two reverse turn slow foxtrot.

Step three reverse turn slow foxtrot.

Feather Finish

The timing of this figure is: slow quick quick.

Man   Rise and fall – rise at the end of step one, up on step two, up and lower at the end of step three.

Lady   Rise and fall – rise at the end of step one, up on step two, up with no foot rise and lower at the end of step three.

Step One

Man   Backing the line of dance, step backwards on the right foot on the toe, lowering the heel, rising back on to the toe, commencing to turn left.

Lady   Facing the line of dance, step forward on the left foot on the heel, rising up on to the toe, commencing to turn left.

Step Two

Man   Step to the side and slightly forward with the left foot on the toe, pointing the toe to the diagonal wall.

Lady   Step to the side with the right foot on the toe, lowering the heel, to end backing the diagonal wall.

Step Three

Man   Step forward on the right foot outside your partner in the contrary body movement position on the toe, lowering the heel, to end facing the diagonal wall.

Lady   Step backwards on the left foot in the contrary body movement position on the toe, lowering the heel, to end backing the diagonal wall.

Step one feather finish
slow foxtrot.

Step two feather finish
slow foxtrot.

Step three feather finish
slow foxtrot.

Three Step

The timing of this figure is: slow quick quick.

Man   Rise and fall – rise at the end of step two, slightly up and lower at the end of step three.

Lady   Rise and fall – rise at the end of step one with no foot rise, up on step two with no foot rise, up and lower at the end of step three with no foot rise.

Step One

Man   Facing the diagonal wall, step forward with the left foot on the heel.

Lady   Backing the diagonal wall, step backwards with the right foot on the toe, lowering the heel.

Step Two

Man   Step forward with the right foot on the heel with a right side lead, rising slightly on to the ball of the foot.

Step one three-step slow foxtrot.

Step two three-step slow foxtrot.

Step three three-step slow foxtrot.

Lady Step backwards on the left foot, toe lowering the heel, no foot rise, with a left side lead.

Step Three
Man Step forward with the left foot, on the toe lowering the heel, continuing a right side lead.

Lady Step backwards with the right foot, on the toe lowering the heel, no foot rise, with a left side lead.

Natural Turn
The timing of this figure is: slow quick quick.

Man Rise and fall – rise at the end of step one, up on step two, up and lower at the end of step three.

Lady Rise and fall – rise slightly at the end of step one with no foot rise, continue to rise on step two, up and lower at the end of step three.

Step One
Man Facing the diagonal wall, step forward on the right foot on the heel, commencing to turn right.

Lady Backing the diagonal wall, step backwards on the left foot on the toe then lowering the heel, commencing to turn to the right.

Step Two
Man Step forward and to the side on the left foot on the toe, backing the line of dance.

Lady Step backwards closing the right foot to the left foot without weight, turning to the right on the left foot, change weight to the right foot (heel turn), to end facing the line of dance.

Step Three
Man Step backwards on the right foot on the toe, then lowering the heel, backing the line of dance.

Step one natural turn slow foxtrot.

Step two natural turn slow foxtrot.

Step three natural turn slow foxtrot.

End of step three showing weight collection before commencing the following step.

Lady Step forward on the left foot on the toe, then lowering the heel, facing the line of dance.

Heel Pull

The timing of this figure is: slow slow slow.
There is no rise and fall.

Step One
Man Backing the line of dance, step backwards on the left foot, commencing to turn to the right on the toe, lowering the heel.

Lady Step forward on the right foot, commencing to turn to the right on the heel, rising up on to the toe.

Step Two
Man Step to the side, with a small step, on the right foot, ending facing the diagonal centre, on the heel and the inside edge of the foot, then the whole of the foot.

Lady Step to the side on the left foot on the toe, then lowering the heel, then on the inside edge of the toe of right foot, ending backing the diagonal centre.

Step Three
Man Step forward on the left foot on the heel, ending facing the diagonal centre.

Lady Step backwards on the right foot, having brushed to the left foot on the toe, then lowering the heel and ending backing the diagonal centre.

You are now in a position to start the routine again: dance steps one to three of a feather step, continuing with steps one to three of the reverse turn, followed by steps one to three of the feather finish, continue with steps one to three of the three step into steps one to three of the heel pull.

From here you can start the improver's routine or continue with the beginner's routine.

To start the improver's steps, continue with the following: steps one to three of a feather step.

Step one heel pull slow foxtrot.

Step two heel pull slow foxtrot.

Step three heel pull slow foxtrot.

IMPROVER'S STEPS

Fallaway Reverse and Slip Pivot

The timing of this figure can be any one of the following:

- slow quick quick slow
- slow quick quick and,
- slow quick and quick,
- slow and quick quick,
- or quick quick quick quick

Man   Rise and fall – rise at the end of step one, up on step two, up and lower at the end of step three.

Lady   Rise and fall – rise at the end of step one with no foot rise, up on step two, up and lower at the end of step three.

Step One
Man   Facing the diagonal centre, step forward on the left foot on the heel, rising up on to the toe and commencing to turn to the left.

Lady   Backing the diagonal centre, step backwards on the right foot on the toe, then lowering the heel.

Step Two
Man   Step forward and to the side on the right foot backing the diagonal wall, moving down the line of dance.

Lady   Step backwards on the left foot in fallaway, backing the diagonal centre and moving down the line of dance on the toe, then lowering the heel.

Step Three
Man   Step backwards on the left foot in the contrary body movement position and fallaway, backing the line of dance on the toe, then lowering the heel.

Lady   Step backwards on the right foot on the toe in the contrary body movement position and fallaway, with a small step, switching hip to end facing the diagonal centre.

Step Four
Man   Step backwards on the right foot, pivoting on the ball of the foot to end facing the line of dance or the diagonal wall, with the left foot held in front of the right foot.

Lady   Step forward on the left foot on the toe, then lowering the heel in the contrary body movement position, pivoting to the centre to end backing the line of dance or the diagonal wall, with the right foot held behind the left foot with no weight.
   Continue to dance steps one to three of a reverse turn.

Reverse Wave
The timing of this figure is: slow quick quick.

Man   Rise and fall – rise at the end of step one, up on step two, up and lower at the end of step three, rise at the end of step five, up and lower at the end of step six.

Lady   Rise and fall – rise slightly at the end of step one with no foot rise, continue to rise on step two, up and lower at the end of step three, rise at the end of step five, up and lower at the end of step six.

Step One
Man   Step backwards with the right foot on the toe, then lowering the heel, backing to the diagonal wall and commencing to turn left.

Lady   Step forward on the left foot on the heel facing the diagonal wall and commencing to turn left.

Step Two
Man   Step backwards on the left foot, curving left towards the line of dance on the toe.

Lady   Step forward on the right foot on the heel, rising up on to the toe.

Step Three
Man   Step backwards on the right foot backing the line of dance on the toe, then lowering the heel.

Lady   Step forward on the left foot facing the line of dance on the toe, then lowering the heel.
   This figure can be continued to a corner of the room, when a heel pull can be danced ready to start the routine again with a feather step.

SLOW FOXTROT MUSIC SUGGESTIONS

- *Witchcraft* by Frank Sinatra.
- *The Way You Look Tonight* by Maroon 5.
- *It Had to be You* by Harry Connick Jr.
- *I've Got You Under My Skin* by Michael Buble.
- *Always* by Bobby Darin.
- *Cheek to Cheek* by Doris Day.
- *Dancing in the Dark* by Barry Manilow.
- *Beyond the Sea* by George Benson.
- *Call Me Irresponsible* by Bobby Darin.
- *Adore You* by Molly Cyrus.

CHAPTER 5

THE QUICKSTEP

The quickstep, as its name implies, is a fast-moving, brisk and energetic dance with the dancers moving elegantly, lightly and quickly around the dance floor. Today's quickstep is characterized by its travelling hops, skips, kicks and flicks. The time signature of the quickstep, like the foxtrot, is 4/4 but, unlike the foxtrot, the tempo or speed of the dance is much quicker at around 50 bars per minute.

In the 1920s the charleston dance reigned supreme. Dance halls were filled with dancers dancing the charleston and the 'quick' foxtrot. As the orchestras played the foxtrot way too fast, two separate dances were developed: the slower foxtrot and the much faster quickstep.

The dance is thought to be English in origin, although some other sources claim it originated in New York, having had its origin in Caribbean and African dances. In either case, the dance captured elements of the quick foxtrot and the charleston, and so the name quickstep was adopted.

The first version of the dance was seen performed by the English couple Frank Ford and Molly Spain at the Star Dance Championship (then the World Championship) in 1927. They danced it without the characteristic knee action of the charleston and so the quickstep, as we dance it today, was born.

Rhythm and expression quickstep.

Beginner's routine quickstep.

Unlike the foxtrot, in the quickstep the man closes his feet, e.g. in the chasses and lock steps. Dancing to an eight-beat count, the timing of the bar is slow, quick, quick, slow, slow (remember a slow is danced to two beats and a quick to one beat of music). Today, advanced figures have further split the beats to form syncopated steps, such as quick and quick and, adding further steps with the 'and' counts. So here we have four steps in just two beats of music.

It is important to note that the walk in the quickstep is different from the walks in either the foxtrot or the waltz. The steps will be shorter as the music is much faster and for this reason there is not the same amount of lowering action as in the waltz and foxtrot dances.

The quickstep is made up of the walk and chasse, and the chasse is included in the basic figure. Having learnt quarter turns, the next figure it is advised to learn is the natural turn, which will be very good groundwork for other figures. Progressive chasse and forward locks would be the next figures to learn, followed by reverse turns. The chasse reverse turn is useful to learn as it is easy to dance in a crowded room. A sound knowledge of basic work before attempting more advanced steps can be enjoyable to dance. A dancer who has mastered the fundamentals of the quickstep will not tire as the quickstep is the most entertaining dance for rhythm and expression.

BEGINNER'S ROUTINE

Quarter Turn to the Right
The timing of this figure is: slow quick quick slow.

Man Rise and fall – commence to rise at the end of step one, continue to rise on steps two and three, up and lower at the end of step four.

Lady Rise and fall – commence to rise at the end of step one with no foot rise, continuing to rise on steps two and three, up and lower at the end of step four.

Step One
Man Facing the diagonal wall, step forward on the right foot on the heel, rising up on to the toe, commencing to turn to the right.

Lady Backing the diagonal wall, step backwards on the left foot on the toe, lowering the heel, no foot rise, commencing to turn to the right.

Step Two
Man Step to the side on the left foot on the toe, turning to the right, backing the diagonal centre.

Lady Step to the side on the right foot, pointing the toe to the diagonal centre.

Step Three
Man Close the right foot to the left foot on the toe, continuing to turn slightly to the right, backing the diagonal centre.

Step one quarter-turn quickstep.

Step two quarter-turn quickstep.

Step three quarter-turn quickstep.

Step four quarter-turn quickstep.

Lady   Close the left foot to the right foot on the toe, facing the diagonal centre.

Step Four
Man   Step to the side and slightly backwards on the left foot on the toe, then lowering the heel, backing the diagonal centre.

Lady   Step diagonally forward on the right foot on the toe, then lowering the heel, facing the diagonal centre.

Progressive Chasse
The timing of this figure is: slow quick quick slow.

Man   Rise and fall – rise at the end of step one, no foot rise, continue to rise on step two and three, up and lower at the end of step four.

Lady   Rise and fall – commence to rise at the end of step one, continue to rise on steps two and three, up and lower at the end of step four.

Step One

Man Backing the diagonal centre, step backwards on the right foot, on the toe, then lowering the heel, commencing to turn left.

Lady Facing the diagonal centre, step forwards on the left foot on the heel, rising up on to the toe.

Step Two

Man Step to the side on the left foot on the toe, pointing the toe to the diagonal wall.

Lady Step to the side on the right foot on the toe, backing the wall.

Step Three

Man Close the right foot to the left foot on the toe facing the diagonal wall.

Lady Close the left foot to the right foot on the toe backing the diagonal wall.

Step Four

Man Step to the side and slightly forward on the left foot, on the toe, then lowering the heel, facing the diagonal wall.

Lady Step to the side and slightly backwards on the right foot, on the toe, then lowering the heel, backing the diagonal wall.

Step one progressive chasse quickstep.

Step two progressive chasse quickstep.

Step three progressive chasse quickstep.

Step four progressive chasse quickstep.

Forward Lock Step

In this routine we are calling it a forward lock, as this is the step that the man is leading. The forward lock and the back lock are given as man and lady, respectively, as the steps are the same.

The timing of this figure is: slow quick quick slow.

Note that this step is normally danced diagonal to the wall. It can be danced forward or backwards for the lady or the man.

Man   Rise and fall – commence to rise at the end of step one, continue to rise on steps two and three, up and lower at the end of step four.

Lady   Rise and fall – the lady does not use foot rise on step one, but rises on step two and three, up and lower at the end of step four.

Step One
Man   Facing the diagonal wall, step forward on the right foot on the heel, rising up on to the toe, outside your partner, in the contrary body movement position.

Lady   Backing the diagonal wall, step backwards on the left foot on the toe, then lowering the heel, in the contrary body movement position.

Step Two
Man   Facing the diagonal wall, step diagonally forward on the left foot on the toe.

Lady   Backing the diagonal wall, step backwards on the right foot on the toe.

Step Three

Man   Facing the diagonal wall, cross the right foot behind the left foot on a toe.

Lady   Backing the diagonal wall, cross the left foot in front of the right foot on a toe.

Step Four

Man   Facing the diagonal wall, step diagonally forward on the left foot on the toe, then lowering the heel.

Lady   Backing the diagonal wall, step diagonally backwards on the right foot on the toe, then lowering the heel.

Step one forward lock step quickstep.

Step two forward lock step quickstep.

Step three forward lock step quickstep.

Step four forward lock step quickstep.

Back Lock Step

Rise and Fall – Man and Lady Commence to rise at the end of step one with no foot rise. Continue to rise on steps two and three. Up and lower at the end of step four.

Step One

Man or Lady Backing the diagonal wall, step backwards with the left foot in the contrary body movement position on a toe, lowering the heel.

Step Two

Man or Lady Step backwards with the right foot on a toe.

Step Three

Man or Lady Backing the diagonal wall, cross the left foot in front of the right foot, on a toe.

Step Four

Man or Lady Backing the diagonal wall, step diagonally backwards with the right foot on a toe, lowering the heel.

Natural Spin Turn

The timing of this figure is: slow quick quick slow slow slow.

Man Rise and fall – commence to rise at the end of step one, continue to rise on steps two and three, lowering the heel at the end of step three. Commence to rise at the end of step four, no foot rise, continue to rise on steps five and six, lowering the heel at the end of step six.

Lady Rise and fall – commence to rise at the end of step one, no foot rise, continue to rise on steps two and three, lowering the heel at the end of step three.

Step One

Man   Facing the diagonal wall, step forward on the right foot on the heel, commencing to turn right.

Lady   Backing the diagonal wall, step backwards on the left foot, toe lowering the heel, commencing to turn right.

Step Two

Man   Step forward ending to the side on the left foot, turning to the right, on the toe, backing the diagonal centre.

Lady   Step to the side on the right foot with the toe pointing to the line of dance on a toe.

Step Three

Man   Close the right foot to the left foot on the toe, lowering the heel of the left foot, backing the line of dance.

Lady   Close the left foot to the right foot on the toe, then lowering the heel of the right foot, facing the line of dance.

Step one natural spin turn quickstep.

Step two natural spin turn quickstep.

Step three natural spin turn quickstep.

Step Four
Man Backing the line of dance, step backwards on the left foot, with the toe turned in to pivot to the right (the right foot is held in front of the left foot without weight).

Lady Facing the line of dance, step forward on the right foot, pivoting action to the right, heel toe.

Step Five
Man Facing the line of dance, step forward on the right foot, on the heel, rising up on to the toe in contrary body movement position, continuing to turn to the right.

Lady Backing the line of dance, step backwards and slightly to the side, on the left foot, on a toe.

Step Six
Man Step to the side and slightly back on the left foot, on the toe, then lowering the heel, backing to the diagonal centre.

Lady Step diagonally forward with the right foot, having brushed the right foot to the left foot, on a toe, lowering the heel

This routine can be continued around the room beginning with steps one to four of the progressive chasse. When the second long side is reached, the improver's steps can then be commenced.

Step four natural spin turn quickstep.

Step five natural spin turn quickstep.

Step six natural spin turn quickstep.

IMPROVER'S STEPS

Start with steps one to six of a natural spin turn, followed by steps one to four of a progressive chasse, continuing with the quick open reverse turn.

Quick Open Reverse Turn

The timing of this figure is: slow quick quick slow.

Man   Rise and fall – rise at the end of step one, up on step two, up and lower at the end of step three.

Lady   Rise and fall – rise at the end of step one with no foot rise, up on step two, up and lower at the end of step three.

Step One
Man   Facing the line of dance, step forward on the left foot, commencing to turn to the left on the heel and rising up on to the toe.

Lady   Backing the line of dance, step backwards on the right foot, commencing to turn to the left on the toe, then lowering the heel.

Step Two
Man   Backing the diagonal wall, step to the side on the right foot, on the toe.

Lady   Step to the side and slightly forward on the left foot, pointing the toe to the line of dance, then moving on to the toe.

Step Three

Man Backing the line of dance, step backwards on the left foot in the contrary body movement position, on the toe, then lowering the heel.

Lady Facing the line of dance, step forward on the right foot in the contrary body movement position and outside your partner, on the toe, then lowering the heel.

Step Four

Man Backing the line of dance, step backwards on the right foot, on the toe.

Lady Facing the line of dance, step forward on the left foot, on a heel.

Four Quick Run

The timing of this figure is: slow quick quick quick quick slow slow.

Man Rise and fall – rise at the end of step one, up on step two, up on step three, up on step four, up on step five, up lowering the heel at the end of step six.

Lady Rise and fall – rise at the end of step one, up on step two, up on step three, up on step four, up on step five, up lowering the heel at the end of step six.

Step One

Man Backing the line of dance, step backwards on the right foot, commencing to turn left on the toe, lowering the heel, then rising up on to the toe.

Lady Facing the line of dance, step forward on the left foot, commencing to turn left on the heel, rising up on to the toe.

Step Two

Man Step to the side and slightly forward on the left foot, pointing it to the diagonal wall, on the toe.

Lady Backing the diagonal wall, step to the side on the right foot, on the toe.

Step Three

Man Step forward on the right foot in the contrary body movement position and outside your partner, facing the diagonal wall, on the toe.

Lady Step backwards on the left foot in the contrary body movement position, backing the diagonal wall, on the toe.

Step Four

Man Step diagonally forward on the left foot, facing the diagonal wall, on the toe.

Lady Step diagonally backwards on the right foot, backing the diagonal wall, on the toe.

Step Five

Man Cross the right foot behind the left foot, facing the diagonal wall, on the toe.

Lady Cross the left foot in front of the right foot, backing the diagonal wall, on the toe.

Step Six

Man Step diagonally forward on the left foot, facing the diagonal wall, on the toe, lowering the heel.

Lady Step diagonally back on the right foot, backing the diagonal wall, on the toe, lowering the heel.

Step Seven

Man Step forward on the right foot in contrary body movement position and outside your partner, facing the diagonal wall, on the heel.

Lady Step backwards in contrary body movement position on the left foot, backing the diagonal wall, on the toe.

Continue with steps one to six of a natural spin turn followed by steps one to four of a progressive chasse and steps one to four of a lock step. Then continue with a fish tail.

Fish Tail

The timing of this figure is: slow quick quick quick quick slow slow.

Man Rise and fall – rise at the end of step one, up on step two, up on step three, up on step four, up on step five, up lowering the heel at the end of step six.

Lady Rise and fall – rise at the end of step one, up on step two, up on step three, up on step four, up on step five, up lowering the heel at the end of step six. When dancing the fish tail diagonally to the wall, there is no turn.

Step One

Man Facing the diagonal wall, step forward on the right foot in the contrary body movement position and outside your partner, on the heel.

Lady Backing the diagonal wall, step backwards on the left foot in the contrary body movement position, on the toe.

Step Two

Man Cross the left foot behind the right foot on the toe.

Lady Cross the right foot in front of the left foot on the toe.

Step Three

Man Step forward and slightly to the side with a small step with the right foot on the toe.

Lady Step backwards and slightly to the side with a small step with the left foot on the toe.

Step Four

Man Step diagonally forward on the left foot with a left side lead, on the toe.

Lady Step diagonally backwards with the right foot with a right side lead, on the toe.

Step Five

Man Cross the right foot behind the left foot, facing the diagonal wall, on the toe.

Lady Cross the left foot behind the right foot, backing the diagonal wall, on the toe.

Step Six

Man Step diagonally forward on the left foot, facing the diagonal wall, on the toe, then lowering the heel.

Lady Step diagonally backwards on the right foot, backing the diagonal wall, on the toe, then lowering the heel.

Step Seven

Man Step forward on the right foot in the contrary body movement position and outside your partner facing the diagonal wall, on the heel.

Lady Step backwards on the left foot in the contrary body movement position, backing the diagonal wall, on the toe.

Tipple Chasse to the Right at a Corner

The timing of this figure is: slow quick quick slow quick quick slow slow.

Man Rise and fall – commence to rise at the end of step one with no foot rise, continue to rise on steps two and three, up on step four, up on step five, up on step six, up lowering the heel at the end of step seven.

Lady Rise and fall – commence to rise at the end of step one, continue to rise on steps two and three, up on step four, up on step five, up on step six, up lowering the heel at the end of step seven.

Step One

Man Backing the line of dance, step backwards on the left foot, commencing to turn right on the toe, then lowering the heel. No foot rise.

Lady Facing the line of dance, step forward on the right foot, commencing to turn right on the heel, then rising up on to the toe.

Step Two
Man Step to the side on the right foot on the toe, turning to face the new line of dance.

Lady Step to the side on the left foot on the toe, turning to back the new line of dance.

Step Three
Man Facing the line of dance, close the left foot to the right foot, on the toe.

Lady Backing the line of dance, close the right foot to the left foot, on the toe.

Step Four
Man Step to the side and slightly forward on the right foot, facing the diagonal wall, on the toe.

Lady Step to the side and slightly back on the left foot, backing the diagonal wall, on the toe.

Step Five
Man Facing the diagonal wall, step diagonally forward with a left side lead, on the toe.

Lady Backing the diagonal wall, step backwards on the right foot with a right side lead, on the toe.

Continue with steps one to four of a forward lock followed by steps one to four of a progressive chasse and steps one to three of a natural turn and steps one to four of a back lock. Then continue with a running finish.

Running Finish

The timing of this figure is: quick quick slow slow or slow quick quick slow.

Man Rise and fall – rise at the end of step one, up on step two, up lowering the heel at the end of step three.

Lady Rise and fall – rise at the end of step one, up on step two, up lowering the heel at the end of step three.

Step One
Man Backing the diagonal wall, step backwards on the left foot in the contrary body movement position, commencing to turn right on a toe.

Lady Facing the diagonal wall, step forward on the right foot, outside your partner in the contrary body movement position on the heel, rising up on to the toe, commencing to turn right.

Step Two
Man Step to the side and slightly forward on the right foot, on a toe, pointing the toe to the line of dance.

Lady Step to the side on the left foot, backing the diagonal centre, on the toe.

Step Three
Man Step forward on the left foot, preparing to step outside your partner, with a left side lead on the toe, lowering the heel, ending facing the line of dance.

Lady Step backwards on the right foot with the right side leading, backing the line of dance on the toe, lowering the heel.

Step Four
Man Facing the line of dance, step forward on the right foot on a heel, in the contrary body movement position, outside your partner.

Lady Backing the line of dance, step backwards on the left foot, on the toe, in the contrary body movement position.

QUICKSTEP MUSIC SUGGESTIONS

• *Sing Sing Sing* by The Benny Goodman Orchestra.

- *That Man* by Caro Emerald.
- *Let's Face the Music and Dance* by Nat King Cole.
- *I'm So Excited* by The Pointer Sisters.
- *Pencil Full of Lead* by Paolo Nutini.
- *As Long as I'm Singing* by Bobby Darin.
- *Go Daddy O* by Big Bad Voodoo Daddy.
- *Puttin' On The Ritz* by Taco.

CHAPTER 6

THE BALLROOM TANGO

Tango was first danced by European émigrés to South America in the 1880s. It was not the same dance that we now call the ballroom or international tango; this dance came far later from Europe.

Back in South America, there was an influx of men into these new countries and they gathered together in the bars and bordellos of Argentina and Uruguay to dance their native dance – tango – after a hard day's work in the pampas. As there were fewer women than men, it was not unusual for men to dance with other men, as well as any available women.

Tango in South America had its roots in the cultures of Africa, native America and early Europe, and instruments like the bandoneon were imported from Germany, as were percussive instruments from Africa.

Today's ballroom tango or international tango branched away from its Argentinian roots with its reintroduction into Europe in the early 1900s – first in Paris, France, then in London and on to other European cities before arriving in New York in 1913.

Like the waltz, tango was seen, back then in

Demonstrates the tango position of body and arms when taking up the ballroom hold, showing that the lady's hand is in a different position than in the other dances.

Europe, as improper and immoral because of its close hold and suggestive movements, and it was somewhat diluted to conform to society's demands. Tango walks were introduced to make it progressive along the dance floor and to make it feel more like a dance.

The dance was popularized in Germany before its eventual introduction to England. In 1922, English dance authorities codified tango for teaching in dance schools and proposed at their conference that it should only be danced to 'modern' orchestral tunes played at around thirty bars per minute (with four beats per bar). The ballroom tango differs from the other three ballroom dances we have covered so far as it has no 'flight' action and its steps are akin to stepping.

The ballroom tango differs from its Argentinian counterpart by having very staccato movements, contrasting slow steps, with quick counts and characteristic head snaps. It has a rhythmic, pronounced and percussively steady beat. It has a time signature of 2/4 with both beats accentuated. There is a very pronounced eight-count beat danced as slow, slow, quick, quick, slow (remember – one beat in a slow and a half-beat for a quick) and travels down the room.

Demonstrates the tango position of the feet. In a closed position, one foot is tucked into the instep of the other foot. This is different from the closed position in the other dances.

Demonstrates the tango position of the man's hand further across the lady's back, which is different from the other dances. Also shows the position of the lady's hand placed just under the man's right upper arm.

The beginner's routine tango.

THE TANGO POSITION AND HOLD

The standing position in tango is also different from the other three dances. You stand with your feet together then move the left foot forward, so that the right foot is tucked into the instep of the left foot.

The lady will be more to the man's right side, but ladies be careful not to go under your man's arm. When the man places his hand on the lady's back, it will be further across the back and the tips of the man's fingers will reach slightly across the lady's spine. The man's forearm should be angled sloping slightly downwards. The lady's left hand should be placed just under the man's right upper arm, being careful not to push her fingers into the armpit, but slightly touching.

THE TANGO WALK

Tango is essentially a walking dance and to dance the tango well, it is essential to be able to walk well. The tango walks are not the same as the steps we have covered so far in the other three ballroom dances and, unlike the other dances, there is no rise and fall in the tango.

The left tango walk is danced in contrary body movement position, while the right tango walk is danced with a right side lead. When walking backwards with the right foot, it is danced in contrary body movement position and when walking backwards with the left foot, this is danced with a left side lead. When danced correctly, the walks will normally curve to the left.

The tango walks are a staccato moving action and the feet are slightly lifted off the floor and placed in position ready for the next step. The back foot is held on the floor for as long as possible, while the front one steps forward. This is totally unlike the gliding action of the other dances.

When stepping forward with the left foot in the contrary body movement position and, considering the curve to the left, do not place the foot across the line of the right foot; it must be placed on the same line of the right foot. This must also be adhered to when walking backwards in the contrary body

movement position with the right foot, which should not be placed across the line of the left foot; it must be on the same line of the left foot.

THE BEGINNER'S ROUTINE

Left Foot Walk

The timing of this figure is: slow.

There is no rise and fall.

Step One

Man   Facing the diagonal wall, step forward on the outside edge of the left foot in the contrary body movement position (this could be considered a slight right-shoulder lead).

Lady   Backing the diagonal wall, step backwards on the inside edge of the right foot in the contrary body movement position (with a slight left-shoulder lead).

Step one left foot walk in tango.

Right Foot Walk

The timing of this figure is: slow.

There is no rise and fall.

Step One

Man Diagonal to the wall, step forward on the inside edge of the right foot, with a right-shoulder lead.

Lady Step backwards on the inside edge of the left foot with a left-shoulder lead.

Progressive Link

The timing of this figure is: quick quick.

There is no rise and fall.

Step One

Man Facing the diagonal wall, step forward on the left foot on a heel in the contrary body movement position.

Lady Backing the diagonal wall, step backwards on the right foot in the contrary body movement

Step one right foot walk in tango.

position on the ball, heel. The turn on the ball of the right foot should be made before the lowering of the right heel.

Step Two

Man Step to the side and slightly back with the inside edge of the right foot and the inside edge of the ball of the left foot, opening to promenade, to end with the body facing the diagonal wall with the left foot pointing diagonal centre.

Lady Step to the side and slightly back with the inside edge of the ball, heel of the left foot and the inside edge of the ball of the right foot, opening to promenade, to end facing the diagonal centre.

This position is when both man and lady are facing and moving in the same direction.

Closed Promenade

The timing of this figure is: slow quick quick slow.

There is no rise and fall.

Step One

Man Diagonal centre, step forward out of promenade on the left foot on the heel in the promenade position.

Lady Diagonal centre, step forward out of promenade on the right foot on the heel in the promenade position.

Step one progressive link in tango.

Step two progressive link in tango.

**Open to promenade
in tango.**

Step Two
Man   Step with the right foot forward and across the left foot in the promenade position and contrary body movement position on the heel.

Lady   Step forward and across the right foot in the promenade position and contrary body movement position on the heel.

Step Three
Man   Step to the side and slightly forward with the inside edge of the left foot.

Lady   Step to the side and slightly back, turning back into the man to a closed position, using the inside edge of the ball then heel of the right foot, to end backing the diagonal centre.

Step Four
Man   Close the right foot to the left foot slightly back, with the whole foot, to end facing the diagonal centre.

Lady   Close the left foot to the right foot slightly forward, with the whole foot, to end backing the diagonal centre.

Step one closed promenade in tango.

Step two closed promenade in tango.

Continue with two tango walks as above and then the open reverse turn.

Open Reverse Turn

The timing of this figure is: quick quick slow quick quick slow.

There is no rise and fall.

Step One

Man Facing the diagonal centre, step forward on the left foot on the heel in the contrary body movement position.

Lady Backing the diagonal centre, step backwards on the right foot, ball heel in the contrary body movement position.

Step Two

Man Step to the side on the right foot, ball heel ending backing the diagonal wall.

Lady Step to the side and slightly forward on the whole of the left foot, pointing down the line of dance.

Step three closed promenade in tango.

Step four closed promenade in tango.

Step Three
Man Step backwards on the left foot, ball, heel in the contrary body movement position, down the line of dance.

Lady Step forward on the right foot, on the heel in the contrary body movement position and outside your partner down the line of dance.

Step Four
Man Step backwards on the right foot, ball, heel, down the line of dance.

Lady Step forward on the left foot on the heel, down the line of dance.

Step Five
Man Step to the side and slightly forward on the inside edge of the left foot, pointing to the diagonal wall.

Lady Step to the side and slightly back on the right foot on the inside edge of ball, heel, backing the diagonal wall.

Step one open reverse turn in tango.

Step two open reverse turn in tango.

Step three open reverse turn in tango.

TOP LEFT: **Step four open reverse turn in tango.**

TOP RIGHT: **Step five open reverse turn in tango.**

RIGHT: **Step six open reverse turn in tango.**

Step Six

Man Close the right foot to the left foot with the whole foot to end facing the diagonal wall.

Lady Close the left foot to the right foot with the whole foot to end backing the diagonal wall.

Continue this routine until you reach the end of the floor, dancing into a corner to the promenade position, and begin the improver's routine.

IMPROVER'S ROUTINE

Natural Promenade Turn

The timing of this figure is: slow quick quick slow.
  There is no rise and fall.

Step One

Man Step to the side on the left foot on the heel
in the promenade position, along the line of dance
pointing to the diagonal wall.

Lady Step to the side on the right foot on the heel
in the promenade position, along the line of dance
pointing to the diagonal centre.

Step Two

Man Facing the diagonal wall, step forward on the
right foot, on a heel in the promenade position and
contrary body movement position.

Lady Step forward and across on a heel in the
promenade position and contrary body movement
position, pointing down the line of dance.

Step Three

Man Step to the side and slightly back on the left
foot on the ball, heel, ball to end backing the line
of dance. (Note: 'ball, heel' is used to explain that
we are not stepping on a toe or a heel directly. The
weight rolls from the inside edge of ball of foot to
the heel.)

Lady Step forward on the right foot, between your
partner's feet, on the heel, down the line of dance.

Step Four

Man Step forward on the right foot in the contrary
body movement position on the heel. The left foot
is placed to the side, without weight, in the promenade position with the inside edge of the foot, to
end facing the diagonal wall of the new line of dance.

Lady Step to the side and slightly back with the
left foot, ball, heel, place the right foot to the side,
without weight, in the promenade position, using

the inside edge of the ball of the right foot to end
facing the diagonal centre.

Five Step

The timing of this figure is: quick quick quick quick
slow, or quick quick slow and slow.
  There is no rise and fall.

Step One

Man Facing the diagonal wall, step forward on the
left foot in the contrary body movement position on
the heel.

Lady Backing the diagonal wall, step backwards
on the right foot in the contrary body movement
position on ball, heel.

Step Two

Man Step to the side and slightly back on the right
foot, turning to back the diagonal wall against the
line of dance, ball, heel.

Lady Step to the side and slightly forward with the
left foot pointing to the diagonal wall against the line
of dance on the whole foot.

Step Three

Man Step backwards with the left foot in the
contrary body movement position, ball heel, diagonal wall against the line of dance. (Note: 'against
the line of dance' means moving in a direction away
from the line of dance.)

Lady Step forward with the right foot in the contrary
body movement position and outside your partner, on
the heel, diagonal wall against the line of dance.

Step Four

Man Step backwards and slightly to the right with
the ball of the right foot, diagonal wall against the
line of dance.

Lady Step forwards and slightly to the left with the
ball of the left foot, diagonal wall against the line of
dance.

Step Five

Man   Place the left foot to the side without weight in the promenade position. Facing the diagonal wall of the new line of dance, lower the heel of the right foot. The inside edge of the ball of the left foot is held still without weight.

Lady   Place the right foot to the side without weight, in the promenade position facing the diagonal centre of the new line of dance. The heel of the left foot is lowered and the inside edge of the ball of the right foot is still held without weight, in the promenade position.

The heel of the man's right foot and the lady's left foot do not lower until the lady has completed her turn.
    Continue with steps one to four of a closed promenade followed by an oversway.

Oversway

The timing of this figure is: quick quick slow slow.
    There is no rise and fall.

Step One

Man   Facing the diagonal centre, step forward with the left foot on a heel, in the contrary body movement position.

Lady   Backing the diagonal centre, step backwards with the right foot, on the ball of the foot, lowering the heel, in the contrary body movement position.

Step Two

Man   Step to the side and slightly back with the right foot on the ball of the foot, lowering the heel to back the line of dance.

Lady   Close the left heel to the right heel with the left toe pointing down the line of dance, whole foot.

Step Three

Man   Step back and to the side, with the left foot, turning the body to face the wall and moving down

and along the line of dance, with the toe of the left foot pointing between the wall and the diagonal wall, with the inside edge of the ball of the right foot, to end still facing the wall.

Lady   Step forward and sideways, turning the body to back the wall, with the right foot, on the ball of the foot, lowering the heel, moving down and along the line of dance, to end backing the wall.

Step Four

Man   Holding the position of step three, flex the left knee pointing the right toe to the diagonal wall against the line of dance, with the inside edge of the ball of the right foot.

Lady   Holding the position of step three, flex the right knee with the left toe pointing to the diagonal centre against the line of dance, with the inside edge of ball of the left foot.

Note – the footwork of the inside edge of the ball of the foot is to allow the heel to lower later.

Drop Oversway

The timing of this figure is: quick quick slow.
    There is no rise and fall.
    This figure can be danced instead of the Oversway; it is more dynamic and adds impact.
    Both Man and Lady dance steps one to three and hold the position, keeping the body still. The man should tilt slightly to the left and the lady to the right. The lady's head will be to the right also. Keeping the feet in place, change abruptly to a right sway for the man, and left for the lady, lowering into the left knee for the man and the right knee for the lady. At the same time the man will be lowering the right shoulder and the lady the left shoulder. The lady will turn her head slightly to the left and the man to the right.

To End the Oversway We Can Open to Promenade

The timing of this figure is: quick quick and slow.
    There is no rise and fall.

Step One

Man Transfer the weight from the left foot to the right foot and place the left foot to the side without weight, to end turning to the promenade position.

Lady Transfer the weight from the right foot to the left foot and place the right foot to the side without weight, to end turning to the promenade position.

(Note: to be in the promenade position without weight means having placed the left foot to the side without weight. We have not stepped on to the foot – it is held in place without weight on it.)

Natural Twist Turn

The timing of this figure is: slow quick quick slow quick quick.
  There is no rise and fall.

Step One

Man Step to the side with the left foot on the heel, in the promenade position, moving along the line of dance pointing to the diagonal wall.

Lady Step to the side with the right foot on the heel, in the promenade position, moving along the line of dance pointing to the diagonal centre.

Step Two

Man Step forward and across with the right foot on the heel in the promenade position and in the contrary body movement position along the line of dance, pointing to the diagonal wall.

Lady Step forward and across with the left foot on the heel, in the promenade position and contrary body movement position, pointing down the line of dance.

Step Three

Man Step to the side with the left foot, on the ball of the foot, then lowering the heel, backing to the diagonal centre.

Lady Step forward with the right foot, between your partner's feet on the heel, down the line of dance.

Step Four

Man Cross the right foot behind the left foot on the ball of the foot, backing the line of dance.

Lady Step forward on the left foot on the heel, preparing to step outside your partner with the left side leading, down the line of dance pointing to the diagonal wall.

Step Five

Man Commence to twist to the right allowing the feet to uncross. Commence on the ball of the right foot and heel of the left foot, towards the diagonal centre.

Lady Step forward on the right foot on the heel ball, in the contrary body movement position, outside your partner.

Step Six

Man Feet are almost closed with weight on the right foot in the promenade position facing the diagonal centre of the new line of dance, with the whole of the right foot and inside edge of the ball of the left foot.

Lady Step to the side, with a small step, with the left foot in the promenade position facing the diagonal centre of the new line of dance on the ball of the foot, then lowering the heel and inside edge of the ball of the right foot.

Continue with steps one to four of a closed promenade followed by a chase.

Chase

The timing of this figure is: slow quick quick quick quick slow.
  There is no rise and fall.

Step One

Man Step to the side in the promenade position with the left foot on the heel, along the line of dance pointing to the diagonal wall.

Lady Step to the side in the promenade position with the right foot on the heel, along the line of dance pointing to the diagonal centre.

Step Two

Man Step forward and across with the right foot on the heel in the promenade position and in the contrary body movement position, along the line of dance, pointing to the diagonal wall.

Lady Step forward and across with the left foot on the heel in the promenade position and in the contrary body movement position, along the line of dance pointing to the diagonal centre.

Step Three

Man Step to the side and slightly forward on the left foot, on the inside edge of ball heel, facing the wall.

Lady Step to the side and slightly back on the right foot on the inside edge of ball heel, backing the wall.

Step Four

Man Step forward on the right foot in the contrary body movement position and outside your partner, ball heel, almost against the line of dance.

Lady Step backwards on the left foot in the contrary body movement position, ball heel, almost against the line of dance.

Step Five

Man Step backwards on the left foot in the contrary body movement position, ball heel, almost diagonal wall.

Lady Step forward on the right foot on the heel and in the contrary body movement position, and outside your partner, almost diagonal wall.

Step Six

Man Step to the side with a small step with the right foot in the promenade position, ball heel and inside edge of the ball of the left foot, facing the diagonal centre.

Lady Step to the side with the left foot. Place the right foot to the side without weight in the promenade position on the ball of the foot, lowering the heel and inside edge of the ball of the right foot, backing the diagonal centre and end facing the diagonal centre against the line of dance.

TANGO MUSIC SUGGESTIONS

- *Blue Tango* by The Joe Loss Orchestra.
- *La Cumparsita* by Danny Malando.
- *Santa Maria (del Buen Ayre)* by Gotan Project.
- *Please Mr Brown* by Alma Cogan.
- *Por Una Cabeza* by The Tango Project.
- *Jealousy* by Alfred Hause and his Orchestra.
- *El Tango de Roxanne* by Ballroom Emotions.
- *Libertango* by Astor Piazzolia.
- *Por Una Cabeza* by Hugo Diaz.
- *Adios Muchachos* by The James Last Orchestra.

CHAPTER 7

BEYOND THE BASICS

To further improve your dance technique it is essential that good balance and posture have been attained. This has been explained in the first part of the book. At this stage, the use of knees comes more to the fore and they must be used correctly and remain soft at all times. Locked-out knees and stiff legs will not allow a good lowering action or allow the weight to be received smoothly.

TRANSFERENCE OF WEIGHT IN THE FORWARD ACTION

Once the walks have been mastered, as referred to in Chapter 2, and balance has been achieved, the steps have become familiar and they are being danced adequately, it is time to discuss the lowering action in more detail: the lowering action for the beginner is only in a walking action, which is really only a slight flexion of the knee. When more advanced dancers start to lower it is far more technical.

Moving on from the walks, stand on either foot with the weight fully committed to this foot. This will now be the standing leg; begin to lower by moving the pelvis forward. This will start to move the weight to the ball of the foot you are standing on and at the same time the shin bone will be lowering towards the floor. It will feel like you are going down an escalator or like a feeling of kneeling down; the centre will now start to move forwards.

Do not have a sitting action, as if going down in a lift. This can be checked out by standing next to a wall and placing a marker where the shoulder is, then start to lower and when doing so the shoulder will move forward from the marker, as the pelvis starts to move forward. Throughout this movement, the body does not move by throwing the weight forward. The body should be kept still and only moves because of the movement through the base. The body must not initiate any of the movement. When maximum lowering is completed, strike the heel of the other foot to the floor. You will now be standing on the ball of the back foot and the heel of the front foot. This is called the middle position.

A test can be done here to check that the weight is in the middle: lower the toe and heel, and turn to the side and if the weight is equally distributed between both of the feet, balance has been achieved. This can be likened to a sumo wrestler stance and this will help in learning the middle position.

Now, having reached the middle position, transfer the weight by immediately putting the toe of the front foot to the floor and moving the pelvis forward in a linear plane. The front knee will flex with the weight still rolling through the back foot as it peels off the floor. While moving across from one foot to the other, try not to push the tummy out, as this will cause the weight to fall backwards.

If the body is either pushed forward or leans forward, the weight will fall forward and the person going backwards will be knocked on to their back foot, and will not be able to transfer their weight correctly.

When practising the lowering action, try not to let the body collapse and drop downwards when commencing to lower. The body should be stretching upwards as the leg is lowering.

LOWERING ACTION WITH EXERCISE BAND

Exercises for this action can be carried out with

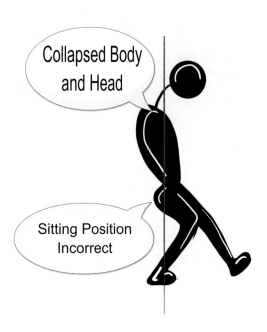

Collapsed Body and Head

Sitting Position Incorrect

Transference of weight in forward action. The illustration demonstrates an incorrect position.

an exercise band that can be obtained from any sports shop. Take the band between your hands, one end at chest height and the other end at pelvis level. When starting to lower, pull the top hand up and the bottom one down; this will enable you to feel your body stretching upwards, as well as feeling grounded on the foot that is pressuring the floor.

The exercise in Chapter 9 for the Achilles' tendon, feet and ankles should be practised, as it is important to have flexible tendons to lower efficiently, and the feet and ankles must be strong.

TRANSFERENCE OF WEIGHT IN THE BACKWARD ACTION

When moving backwards with a lowering action, start by moving the hip of the standing leg backwards. The hip moves away from the knee but the knee does not move forward over the toe. Do not lower vertically by pushing the posterior out. Try to have a feeling of going backwards down the esca-

lator or, as mentioned in Chapter 2, the walking action, sitting on a seat. Now, reaching the middle position, being on the ball of the back foot and the heel of the front foot, move the pelvis backwards. As this happens, the back knee flexes forward and the front leg straightens, releasing the toe from the floor. This leg will now move towards the back foot, skimming the floor with the ball of the foot. Do not throw the body weight backwards by moving the body because this will cause you to go off-balance. The same exercise can be used here with the exercise band. The front foot will feel as if it is pressuring into the floor and the body will be stretching upwards.

Having described the transference of weight from foot to foot and discussed the middle position, it is also important to state that you must try to roll the weight evenly through the foot. It is advisable to try to correct any rolling over to the side of the foot causing the balance to be disturbed.

If there is still difficulty in understanding how to move from the legs and not the body, liken it to a spider: true, it has eight legs and we only have two. Watch the spider and how it moves its legs, reaching out into a position before it puts the weight on it. Its body is only transported by its legs; it does not move the body independently. The leg must be in position before the body, so as to be able to

EXERCISE FOR BACKWARD ACTION

The following exercise will help with the backward action:

Place a chair with the back to a wall, stand to the side of the chair towards the front end with your standing leg against the seat. Now, without the knee coming forward, sit down. The free leg must be held back and allowed to move; do not put any weight on to this leg. A feeling of moving backwards through the hip should be experienced.

receive the body weight. Keep in mind that the legs split and the weight is then moved across through the legs.

MOVING UP ON TO A TOE FROM A HEEL

When moving up on to a toe from a lowering step, as you transfer your weight through the foot you are arriving on to, continue to rise up through the foot, as well as pulling up through the core of the body. Using the exercise band, place it around the back of the neck and hold the ends, one in each hand. As you are rising up on to the toe, pull down on the band and feel the body rising upwards. The toe will be pressuring into the floor.

PULLING TO THE BACK OF THE CIRCLE

Start in a practice hold and imagine a hoop, or use a hula hoop, around both partners at waist level. Inside this circle, both partners should pull to the back of the hoop with the lower back and try to find a connection to each other. Try to dance a forward walk and then a backward one, maintaining this pull to the back of the hoop. When doing this exercise, the transverse muscles are being

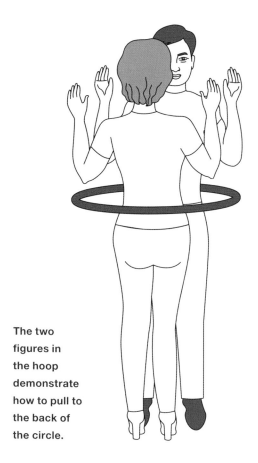

The two figures in the hoop demonstrate how to pull to the back of the circle.

contracted. This gives a feeling of pulling the belly button to the back of the spine.

This can also be practised with the palms of both hands at shoulder height held to your partner. The hands will be in the middle of the partnership.

TRACKING OF THE FEET AND LEGS

Movement of the feet and legs requires dancing on two tracks most of the time. Some steps are across or on the same line. In tango, there are some steps that are danced on one track. Dancing on two tracks means that, when stepping backwards or forward, the foot should not cross the other foot's track, unless the step requires this; loss of balance will occur if it does. The feet should always pass underneath the body and not splay out to the side. The tops of the legs should come together, rather than having a space between them. The foot should pass

TRY THIS EXERCISE

Begin by contracting the transverse abdominal muscles pulling the tummy to the back of the spine and feeling for the connection to the partner through the hands. Again, try to walk and maintain this position.

Try to use this technique in all of your dancing to maintain a constant flow of movement. When using this technique, it allows a freedom of movement, rather than having a rather 'stuck on' feeling to the partner.

the other foot closely, almost touching the inside edge of the ball of the foot, where the shoes sometimes will wear out. Ladies should track the inside of the man's right leg and the same applies for the man who must track the inside of the lady's leg. It is also very important to keep the feet straight and not turn them outwards or inwards, unless the step requires us to do so. Try to avoid the turn out of the feet as in Latin dancing. The feet should remain parallel at all times to allow for the correct rolling action of the feet from heel to toe and toe to heel. To get the best

Man's poise in the hold. The photo shows the man's and the lady's perfect balance and how the weight is dropping downwards through the spine.

foot and ankle usage, always line up your foot to the direction of travel.

The term pointing the toe is used to indicate the next direction we are dancing to. A good example of this is the feather finish in the foxtrot where the man steps backwards with his right foot and points his left toe to the next alignment.

ADVANCE PREPARATION STEP

The Preparation Step is a step taken to prepare the couple to start dancing. It is not a figure. The reason for this step is to make sure that the couple are on the correct foot and balanced, and so perform a smooth transition into the first step of their routine. It is used to start the Waltz, Foxtrot, and Quickstep. The timing and alignments will be different in each dance, but the movement is the same.

Example of Foxtrot Preparation Step
The timing for this step is: slow, slow, slow.

The couple will start in a closed position, Man facing diagonal centre, Lady backing diagonal centre.

Step One
Man Step to the side with the left foot, on the inside edge of the foot continuing onto whole foot, taking a wide step. The body turns to the right.

Lady Step to the side on the right foot. The body turns to the right.

Step Two
Man Step to the side with the right foot, on the inside edge of the foot continuing onto whole foot, taking a wide step, and brush the left foot to the right foot. The body then turns to the left.

Lady Step to the side with the left foot, on the inside edge of the foot continuing onto whole foot, brushing the right foot to the left foot.

Step Three
Man Step forward with the left foot on a toe lowering the heel, Diagonal to Centre.

Lady Step back on the right foot on a ball lowering the heel.

THE MAN'S POISE IN THE HOLD

The man should stand tall, shoulders pulled down the back, and have a vertical weight fall. He should present a strong right side to the lady. The head should be slightly to the left; do not lift the chin up to try to grow tall, instead push the feet down into the floor, giving you a feeling that your upper body is rising upwards through the ribcage. Again, do not try to lift the chest upwards, as this will result in you concaving the lower back and cause you to end up with back ache. The elbows should not be pulled back behind the shoulders: the left elbow should be in line with the shoulder and not exaggerated forward, as this will push the lady's arm behind her back.

The man's frame should allow the lady's elbows and arm to be in line with her shoulders.

THE LADY'S POISE IN THE HOLD

The lady's poise in dancing is not easily attained, so in the beginner's section (*see* Chapter 2 under the heading Attaining the Ballroom Dancer's Hold) we discussed only the stance with the lady's right side to the man's right side. The lady's elbows and right upper arm should be in line with her shoulders and the man's hold should be correct to allow for this.

Having now been dancing for some time and having attained some understanding and progress in the technique of taking hold with a partner, start in the same hold, right side to your partner's right side and, without turning the right side off the man, rotate the left side towards the man. To help you feel this action, a good exercise to try is to stand in front of the mirror and, without turning your head, feet or hips, turn the body to the right. You should feel a twisting spiral feeling in the body. Taking hold again, try to emulate the feel of this exercise, only do not move the right side away from the man's right side. The feeling should be one of a natural extension in the head to the left, and a lifting of both sides of

the ribcage. This will cause a twisting feeling in the mid-section of the body like a spiral, keeping the right hip towards the man; the head will then project outwards and slightly to the left by the rotation of the body underneath the head, like the feeling from the exercise. Do not turn the head to the left, as this will cause a look of a stiff neck; the above action will angle the head and it will look softer.

There should be no leaning backwards from the waist, as this will cause the body to be back weighted. The lady should extend backwards from just under the shoulder blades. Having discussed the use of the transverse muscles, the lower back should not concave. Any extension from the lower back and waist will stop the legs from being able to move. A correct lowering action will not be achieved and the leg will be prevented from moving out before the body, consequently the legs will be chasing after the body in a falling backwards motion that is out of control, instead of being able to transfer the weight as described. You will not be able to stop efficiently and will be off-balance. The lady should maintain her vertical weight fall, otherwise the man may feel that the lady is heavy.

Connection
- The lady should have a good connection with the man's hip, which monitors his rise and fall.
- A connection with the man's ribcage monitors his shaping. Shaping is discussed on page 123.
- Connection with the man's right thigh and the lady's right thigh monitors movement.

The Lady's Right Side
Ladies must always be aware of their right side. It must be strong, in as much as it should always stay towards the man and be closed to the man, except in counter steps. When trying to achieve this, the lady must still maintain her centre to the man.

Keeping a right side is not as easy as it sounds and in advanced dancing it is very important if you are trying to achieve a better standard of dancing. One example of this is when turning to promenade. A common mistake in this step is when the ladies open up their right side completely, causing

Extension in lady's lines.

a strain on the partnership, and resulting in the left side closing up, which now reduces the space in the hold. This will result in displacing the man by pulling him forward and off-balance. The V-shape that has been discussed in Chapter 2 is in the base – the hip area, in this position – as the lady's hip should be situated behind the man's hip.

So How Is a Strong Right Side Achieved?

First, we must have an awareness of our right side and then be able to use the feet, legs and hips to maintain it. So ladies, taking the promenade position as an example, when coming out of promenade with the right leg, and lowering to step through with the left leg, there should be a feeling of the right side coming towards the left knee.

If going into a chasse from promenade, the lady closes back to the man and this is done by turning the hip and not the body. If the body turns as well as the hip, the lady will end up under the man's right arm in a square position. If the hip alone turns, a right side will be maintained to the man. Ladies must be aware of the steps that turn back to close to the man. Some examples of these are the chasse and weave from the promenade position.

When trying to keep a right side, ladies must be aware that they must not push or attach themselves on to the man, thereby restricting the movement and space for both parties. In attempting to keep a right side, think of achieving this by using the legs more and not by trying to keep up with the man by pushing the right side into him and leaving the legs behind, looking as though running after the man with the top part of the body only. It is a very soft contact that should be felt and not a hard one. A lady's left side must not be allowed to drop or pull away in the attempt to keep the right side; the left side should be lifted.

EXTENSION IN THE LADY'S LINES

When discussing the lady's hold position, it was pointed out that there should be no leaning backwards from the waist. This also applies to the lady's extension in the lines.

Using the contra check as an example of extension in the lady's lines, the lady steps back in contrary body movement position with her right foot. The steps has one eighth of a turn with the body turning more with her weight split between both legs. The lady now has to extend her line and this is achieved by a forward movement, not a backward one. Having taken step one, the man steps forward with his left foot in the contrary body movement position and the lady steps backwards with the right foot in the contrary body movement position. Both parties have a right side to each other and are moving diagonally backwards. Now having completed the step, the lady holds her ribcage to the right side of the man. The left side of the ribcage should not drop or pull in a backward direction. There should be no leaning backwards, as this could pull the man over. The left side should remain up and forward; the lady's body is diagonally up towards the man. The lady should not pull backwards away from the man in the attempt to make a bigger extension. The head will extend and the neck should be stretched. The neck should not form a C-shape causing the head to tip backwards and become very heavy. The head should not be in a position where the lady is looking at the ceiling with her chin upwards. The lady's head should be in alignment with her right foot and should not be extending out beyond the right foot.

The lady may feel a slight rotation as the man changes his shape from the left to the right. If this happens in a line figure like the contra check, and the lady takes her head weight backwards at the same time as stepping backwards, she will pull the man off-balance.

CENTRES

The Man's Centre to the Lady

Having studied the hold, and the man and the lady's right side, an awareness of centres is also important. The man should turn the centre of his body from the solar plexus (base of the sternum) slightly towards the lady, but should not be turning inside his own arm, as this will cause a problem in the hold and decrease the lady's space. The man's solar plexus

The man's centre to the lady showing correct position. The centre is the point where the solar plexus is situated, which is the bottom of the ribcage.

An incorrect position of the centres being turned away from each other and causing the partners to end up under each other's arms and body contact to be lost.

is towards his right hand. The right hand will have a feeling of moving away and not one of pulling the lady inwards, thereby cutting down the space in the right arm. We have to maintain this centre throughout the whole of dancing except in certain positions when the bodies change sides in a counter position. An example of this is when the man moves left side to the right side of the lady and vice versa. Having achieved the centre between the couple, it is important not to open the left side, because if this happens, you will lose the centre.

The Lady's Centre to the Man

The lady basically does the same as the man in turn-

ing her solar plexus towards him; now both centres are towards each other. When turning the solar plexus, the right side must not turn away – it is similar to the hold when feeling a twist inside the body. The right ribcage is held to the right side of the man and the left is held forward by the back muscles (latisimus dorsi) and should feel as though they are moving inwards and upwards towards the right side. The right side is held and the left comes around.

Centres to Each Other

Holding the centre to each other is crucial to maintaining a connection. If the centre is turned away from the partner, it is likely they will dance underneath the armpit in a square position, and all leading and following will be lost. As will be discussed in the following two paragraphs, the solar plexus is turned towards the partner and it is held there for the duration of the dance.

The Common Centre

The common centre is where the balance of the partnership is; we have our own balance and the balance of the couple. The common centre is in the space between the centre of the man and lady.

DIRECTION OF WEIGHT

Commencing to turn at the beginning of a step will cause the weight to be danced straight into the partner. This will cause the partnership to go off-balance. We must always dance with our centres towards each other and this does not change when directing the weight past our partner. Commencing to turn at the end of the step allows us to dance our weight past our partner without losing the centres; your weight will now be directed past your partner and not into him/her.

The space to the right side of the man's head is what is sometimes referred to as the 'lady's window' and the space to the lady's right side of her head is the 'man's window'. Both partners now have a space to dance into without disturbing the common centre. So with this in mind, commence to turn at the end of the step and there should be a feeling of dancing past the partner by directing the body weight through the window. This is explained in more detail, and perhaps could be understood better, in the section Inside and Outside of Turns, later in this chapter.

THE HEAD WEIGHT

The human head is very heavy and if used incorrectly, it will unbalance us. When dancing, the head should remain still, unless it is used intentionally to aid a step. The head weighs approximately between 10 and 11lb (4.5–5kg). This being the case, it is important what dancers do with their heads and

the effect it can have on how the couple moves. Holding our posture in a correct vertical stance, with the head directly aligned on top of the spine, we are on balance. The weight will be evenly distributed down the body and the spine will not have stress put upon it.

Any movement made with the head can affect this balance. The body can be pulled in a direction that we did not intend to go. Dancers can be quite challenged by this, as they need to keep the alignment of the head over the spine, while moving and making shapes and lines. Using their head incorrectly will affect their dancing in a negative way.

It is a common error in dancing to bring the head forward; this adds weight to the front of the body, pulling the dancer off-balance. When the head is in front of the spine, the body's alignment is no longer perfectly balanced. Even if it is only slightly forward, it will restrict us from using our standing leg, preventing any drive forward. Looking down will take the head weight forward, so try not to do this.

When the head is angled forward, it will start to move the upper part of the body forward, instead of being able to engage the pelvis and legs. You will be falling into the step, off-balance and out of control, as the body tries to stay upright by chasing the weight. This means that you are moving faster and faster to try and catch yourself.

When walking backwards, if the head is behind the spine, again the body will be out of control and the action will speed up as the feet try to stop the body from falling.

In positions where the head is turned, e.g. in the promenade position, the position of the head, as well as timing of the head turn, are important. If the head turns too fast or is tipped forward or backwards, it will affect the couple's balance. If the head is turned to the ceiling by shortening the neck, it will pull the partner off-balance, especially in steps that are rotating.

In backward steps, if the head is taken back before the leg is extended into position, it will put the head behind the spine. If this happens in a step like the contra check and the lady takes her head with her foot when stepping backwards, she will pull the man off-balance. The foot must be in position before the head is extended.

Some steps and lines will cause the spine to be at an angle; in these positions the head should also be angled in the same direction to keep the line of the spine from the top of the head through the spine, but there must always be a foot behind to balance the body.

Moving the head from side to side will also affect the balance of the couple, so try to keep the head still and use your peripheral vision to maintain good floor craft.

The Use of Head Weight

When moving backwards in natural turning figures, the head remains still and the body turns first underneath the head. This will create a bigger extension to the left.

When moving backwards in reverse turning figures, the head will start the lead of the turn, and not the body, otherwise the man will be pulled and at the end of the turn the body will be too straight. An example would be the double reverse spin. In other figures where the body sways, the head stays still.

After an extension of the head at the end of the figure, the head comes back to neutral. The lady should not try to maintain a constant extension. Also, the lady should not pull on the man's arm while trying to extend, as this will distort the frame.

Both the man and the lady should keep their heads in their own space and not cross over into each other's space. Promenade position is a step where the lady has to stay behind the man's hip, so she should keep her head weight to the left, although the head turns to the right.

Understanding Head Weight

Head weight is not normally discussed until after a few years of dancing, so even if the dancer is not yet ready to apply it to their dancing, an understanding of it at an earlier stage may help you in the future. In trying to understand head weight, we can think of an oval shape. Divide the oval into four quarters and imagine the man in the left quarter at the bottom of the oval with his head to the left and stretched diagonally backwards, away from the centre of the oval. The lady is diagonally opposite in the top quarter of the oval with her head to the left and stretched diagonally backwards, away from the centre of the oval. Now imagine being in a hold: the man's right forearm is in the same quarter of the oval as the lady, with his hand on her back. The lady's right arm is in the quarter of the oval beside her. The man's right upper arm and the lady's left forearm are in the quarter of the oval beside the man to his right. As previously mentioned, try to imagine the man has a window to the right of the lady and the lady has a window to the right of the man.

The lady's posture and extension, as well as her head weight, are important during rotation and extension in lines and can be used as a counterbalance to maintain balance. Referring back to the oval, both partners' head weight should be on the outside of the edge of the oval and this should be maintained throughout the dancing to hold the counterbalance.

The man's head weight should stay in his side of the oval and lady's in hers. Where the man's head weight dances, the lady's head weight must go diagonally across to the opposite side of the man's. In general, the man stays in his quarter of the oval and the lady in her quarter most of the time, but there are exceptions to this rule. In natural figures with rotation to the right, the man will stretch forward to the quarter of the oval to the right of the lady, which is the opposite to him (imagine stretching through the window); this encounters contrary body movement as well, but the head must stay to the outside of the large oval and must not go straight forward or into the lady. This would be executed at the end of step one of a natural turn in the waltz, and in the feather step in the foxtrot at the end of step one.

On turns to the left, the man must stay in position, maintaining the head weight to the centre of the small oval; it will be the man's centre that travels around the partner on the large oval. The man should not try to do the opposite of the above and stretch to the quarter to the man's right, as this will cause you to be off-balance in the turn and lose your positioning to each other.

In some figures, e.g. the throwaway oversway and the left whisk, the man will bring his head weight back and around to the quarter of the oval to his right, and the lady will be back and around to the quarter of the oval to her right.

In the contra check figure, the man steps straight through the centre of the oval into the lady's quarter of the oval and it would be impossible for the lady to go in the opposite direction, as she is stepping backwards. The lady's head weight will be sent backwards but her body weight must be sent in a forward direction diagonally upwards towards the man.

The collection of the foot under the body before taking the next step is an important action to acquire for control and balance.

Learning to use your base correctly is essential to being a good dancer.

When practising, try to obtain and maintain a counterbalance, thinking of the head weight and the oval, and using the window analogy – whichever works best.

COLLECTION

Collection is the point when the moving leg comes into the side of the standing leg. This happens at the end of the step.

On all steps, the moving leg should always move under the body before continuing to the next position. The moving leg should not move out to the side like a straddle position, leaving a space between the legs. It should move into the standing leg or move past the standing leg on its way to another step.

Collection is about the legs passing underneath the body and this should happen throughout dancing to keep control and balance. The moving leg starts on its way to the next position by passing under the body.

SHAPING

When shaping to the right as a man in the natural turn in the waltz, we are commencing to turn to the right by using contrary body movement. Do not allow the left shoulder to swing forward and the right shoulder to go in a backward direction, as this will impair the movement going forward. The right side still has to move in a forward direction. Think of the right side of the ribcage dancing through the lady's right ribcage. Do not drop either side of the body when shaping. An exercise to help with the shaping is already explained in the section The Lady's Poise in the Hold. The feeling that you should get from this exercise is the one that you want to try and feel when shaping to either the left or the right.

COMMENTS ON THE USE OF THE BASE

It is our base that moves us around the dance floor. Our body remains still on top of the base and does not dance, as such. The body is used for shaping and, in certain positions; for example, some are contrary body and outside your partner's position, rotation and extension in the lines.

Learning to use your base correctly is imperative to being a good dancer, and it has been mentioned previously about the body moving in front of the legs, causing a falling and a chasing of the weight, with the feet trying to catch up. Moving the body to the music and trying to express the music with the body may feel very nice but it causes many problems and makes dancing look heavy, cumbersome and untidy. Dancing is stillness in motion, with the motion coming from the base. The expression can be seen in the lines and shaping, and interpretation of the music through the way the choreography is performed.

One of the consequences of moving the body weight with the foot is being out of control, which could lead to bumping into other couples on the dance floor because of the inability to stop. When the man's weight is forward of his body, the lady will feel under pressure to move away with her weight being knocked on to her back foot, the effect being like a pinball action, and now both partners are moving in an uncontrolled movement. This problem will not allow the couple to transfer weight together in a smooth movement.

Even more dangerous is when a man moves his body weight forward in lines such as the contra check and the throwaway oversway. When the man is stepping into a contra check, his head should be aligned over the spine and not forward of it. This again will push the body weight forward and could result in falling over or putting a strain on the lady's back. The weight should be held in the space that is the centre of gravity between the couple. The lady's head should also be aligned with her spine and, although she is extending her head and the top part of her body backwards, her leg is extended well past her head position, allowing her to remain on balance. If the lady, when stepping backwards, throws her body weight and head weight backwards, she could pull the man over. Any forward motion or backward throwing of the weight will result in loss of balance. The foot must be in position first and the weight then transferred on to it.

The centre of gravity of the body has to fall directly over the base (in dancing, the base is referred to as the lower half of the body, i.e. from the hips to the feet) and will pull the centre of balance downwards. The base is the structure that will support you and allow you to be perfectly balanced.

Dynamic Balance

Dynamic balance is mostly used in dancing because there is movement. Momentum and gravity act on the body in different directions, so the centre and the base must be in alignment with those directions. For example, let's look at the natural turn in the waltz for the man. Between steps one and two, the man is in a sway position. On step one, movement is produced from the driving action, on step two he is affected by gravity and momentum, and his base has to be between these two forces. To stay on balance, technical sway is used. This is an

Static balance – the spine is in a straight line with the weight dropping down; the centre of gravity has to fall directly over the base.

BALANCE IN MORE DETAIL

Static Balance

Static balance is achieved when the following parts of the body are lined up correctly when standing still:

- Head
- Shoulders
- Ribcage
- Pelvis
- Legs
- Feet

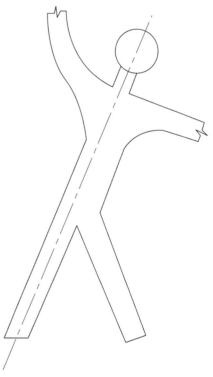

Dynamic balance – this is an inclination of the body away from the direction of movement, but the spine remains straight on the inclination.

inclination of the body away from the direction of movement; this is dynamic balance and when arriving on the foot at the end of step two, the sway helps him to stop, and on step three this is static balance. Balance is when the centre of mass is over the foot. If you danced a natural turn in the waltz holding your body straight up and down, and tried to put in momentum without sway, you would fall over, as the momentum would cause you to carry on moving past where you wanted to stop. To be dynamically balanced, control is needed of where your weight is, in respect to multiple forces acting upon you.

BALANCE OF MOVEMENT

Balance of movement is achieved by feeling where the core is and where the centre of gravity is. The centre of gravity is about three inches below the navel. The tops of the legs can be considered to be a centre-of-gravity point; this puts the balance in between the hips and bottom. The better you can start the movement from here, the more efficient the movement will be. Along with a better understanding of our centre of gravity and how to move our weight correctly, before, during and after our movement, is the beginning of a smooth and controlled weight transference from foot to foot.

The term base is often used in dancing terms and the initiation of movement is from this lower part of the body only, from the waist down. The hips are where the power is generated; the pelvis/hips lead the leg movement. Other muscles that connect the pelvis to the lower part of the body are the gluteus maximus, which are in the buttocks, and the psoas muscles, which are either side of the navel; these muscles are involved in stabilizing the spine through their connection to the pelvis and tops of the thighs. Any forward stepping movement should be propelled from the hips and not the body or head.

Skilful weight transference is the key to solid balance and is efficient, and enables the movement to be smooth. There has been much research done on this in training on fall prevention. Perseverance is the key here, so constant practice of the lowering action and transferring of the weight is vital.

It does not require much effort to pay attention to weight transference in all activities throughout the day and you will soon be aware of the changes you have achieved in your movements. Better movement improves performance in all activities. It is a very different feeling having achieved control in every step performed in dancing, compared to guess work and feeling unsure.

When dancing, try to be aware of where the core and centre of gravity are, and do not forget what has been discussed in the balance section of the book on the vertical weight fall. Remember, do not throw the body weight from side to side or backwards and forward. Motion before movement is felt from the centre of gravity being moved forward or backwards from the pelvis, which initiates the leg movement. Practising the forward and backward walks will help acquire this feeling.

THE BALANCE OF THE COUPLE

Individual balance has already been covered in Chapter 2, and hopefully you have worked on the exercises and achieved this. Without your own individual balance, there will be no chance of achieving the balance of the couple.

Having already discussed the centres of the couple and that they are always angled towards each other, unless the step dictates otherwise as in counter positions, the need for a common centre is necessary. A common centre allows us to dance together on balance. This common centre is where the centre of the weight of the couple is, so we now have an individual weight fall and the weight fall of the couple.

Stand facing your partner about one foot apart with arms to the sides. Have a sense of the centres towards each other and envisage a third centre between you and your partner – this is the common centre. The common centre is vertical and should remain stable and calm. Any constant movement of the head from side to side or the body will unsteady the centre of balance of the couple. The centre is held and we do not lead with it. In the hold, the man presents his arms to the common centre and not towards his own centre.

The lady should not try to feel light as this will have the opposite effect and make her feel heavy. When trying to be light the body is lifted and therefore does not have a feeling of the weight dropping downwards; this makes it difficult for the man to feel where the lady is. The fingers of the lady's hand should hang over the man's hand with a feeling of a weight fall, but do not pull downwards on the hand.

When achieving the weight fall between the couple, you will feel very much attuned to the partner and where each other's weight is, and leading and following will be easily maintained.

THE EYES

Eyes are important in assisting us in controlling movement. The vestibulo–ocular reflex connects the eye to the rest of the body. The head has a connection to the brain to follow the eyes, and the body has a connection to the brain to follow the head. You can test this out by moving your head in different directions and the body will follow. In dancing, the eyes are important – they should be looking in the direction of travel but this is not always the case, as we are often stepping backwards; therefore, we should not try to look behind us, as this will pull the partnership in another direction to the one we are trying to travel in.

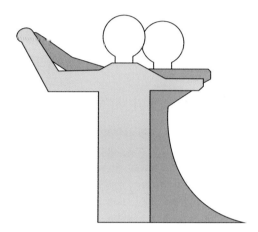

The shoulders should be parallel in dancing poise.

SHOULDERS PARALLEL

The man should raise his elbows so that they are parallel to the floor. It would be acceptable to have a slight downward position to make a smooth line with a slight curve from the neck to elbows. If a man is dancing with a lady much shorter than himself, he must lower the elbows to accommodate her.

The man should have a straight line from his right shoulder to his left elbow. The right elbow is slightly forward of the left elbow, which will also help with a right-side connection to the lady; also, this will create space for the lady to settle in. The man would have to increase or decrease this space to the size of the lady he is dancing with. The man should not pull his right arm in towards his own body. He should not allow his elbows to rise above his shoulders.

The lady's shoulders should be parallel to the man's shoulders and her elbows should never fall below her shoulder line. Her upper arms should be parallel to the floor. The lady should have a straight line from the right shoulder to the left elbow; this will likewise help with a right-side connection to the man. The right arm should have a soft curve that is forward of the shoulder, so her hand can rest on the man's hand. Her left hand is placed on the man's upper right arm by the deltoid muscle.

Common Mistakes

Man:
- Dropping of the elbows causes a look of bad posture.
- Lifting of the shoulders causes the back to look hunched.
- Lifting the elbows and keeping the shoulders down requires practice and it might help to do some shoulder exercises to assist you in this (*see* Chapter 9).
- Left elbow too far forward. The man should have a straight line from right shoulder to left elbow. If the left elbow moves too far forward, it causes the lady to open her right side, which looks unnatural and is incorrect.

- Right elbow too far back. The right elbow should always be in front of the man's body. If the man tries to have a straight line from elbow to elbow, he will decrease the space for the lady.

Lady:
- Hanging on the man. The lady must have a vertical weight fall, as has been discussed previously, but she must not pull down on the man's hand or rest her weight on his right arm.
- The lady's left elbow must be at shoulder level or higher; it must not sag downwards, as it will spoil the top line.
- The lady should not take her right side away from the man, as her shoulders will not stay parallel. It may be that the man may have his left arm too far forward, causing this problem.

RISE AND FALL IN THE WALTZ

Rise and fall is a very important aspect in the waltz, which gives the waltz its pendulum look. Rise and fall should have a smooth flow and not a sharp rise on beat two. Considering the first three steps of a natural turn for the man and steps four to six for the lady, and dancing a preparation step on step three: the weight is on the left foot, commence to roll the weight through the foot and release the left heel. The body weight will continue to move forward, at the same time the right foot should move forward on a ball in contact with the floor. Step heel toe and arrive in the middle position, weight split between both legs; the ball of the back foot will still have pressure in it. Flex the right knee to allow the weight to arrive on the right foot. Continue to roll through the toe of the back foot commencing to rise. The left foot swings through, and at the same time the right knee will straighten, continuing to rise smoothly. The left foot swings forward, ending to the side on a toe with the weight between both feet with pressure into the right foot. Close the feet together still rising. The legs will now be held with knees slightly flexed, they should not be locked out. There will be a change of weight on beat three to the right foot. Lower the heel of the right foot. Do not lower the heel and flex the knee at the same time. The heel must be lowered first and then the knee will flex for the lowering of the next step. The left leg will be extending backwards without weight on the ball of the foot in preparation for the next step. When changing weight to the right foot, and using the correct technique, allow the weight to drop by relaxing the legs.

When dropping the weight quickly, speed is created and levels out as the momentum continues to move us forward before the rise. By using the fall of weight, gravity will work for you, allowing the action to be more fluid.

INSIDE AND OUTSIDE OF TURNS NATURAL AND REVERSE

On any turn to the left or to the right, one partner is on the inside of the turn and the other on the outside of the turn. The person on the inside of the turn is pulling to the centre of that turn and the partner on the outside of the turn will be dancing past the one on the inside.

The partner stepping forward is on the outside of the turn, while the partner stepping backwards is on the inside of the turn. The partner on the outside of the turn is moving further than the one on the inside. When on the outside of the turn, the contrary body movement of the body will be towards the moving foot at the end of the step. There should be no tipping of the shoulders and no moving a shoulder forward or the opposite one back, as this would cause a pushing or pulling in the partnership. When stepping backwards, the contrary body movement is at the end of the step; this will allow the partner going forward to move past. This should create a feeling of – you go, then I go.

There should be a feeling of dancing through the partner and not around the partner. For example, on a natural turn in the waltz, the man on step one would step straight through the lady's right shoulder with his right side. At the end of the step, he would put in contrary body movement and he would swing past the lady. If the man tries to go around his partner and turns too early, he will not be able to swing

past the lady and he will dance straight into his partner and lean into the turn, causing his partner to be pushed off-balance.

Natural and Reverse Turns

To explain natural and reverse turns, and to be able to understand them more easily, an explanation in terms of small and large circles can be of help, although, as most rotational figures travel as well as rotate, it will not resemble a circle but more of an oval shape. Stand with your partner and imagine a triangle with the base of the triangle at your feet, and the common centre being the top. Then imagine your top lines spreading out like a fan and your heads at opposite ends of the fan. Imagine now spinning around the common centre and your heads moving around in a big circle. The individual centre will be close to the common centre and will be a small circle. Imagine the lady holding her head in one position while the man rotates clockwise around her head. The lady's head is the centre of rotation; her body is rotating around the central point in a larger circle. The man is connected to the lady with his centre to her centre and his body will be going around her head; but his head is a long way from her head, instead his head will be travelling in a large circle compared to his body. The lady will be making a small circle with her head as it is in a fixed position, while her body is the big circle. The man's body is rotating around the centre in a small circle and his head in a big circle.

When rotating together, there will be two circles, a small one and a big one. The centre will follow the one circle and the head weight the other. For example, the natural turn in the waltz steps one to three for the man and four to six for the lady. When stepping forward and rotating to the right, the head weight will be to the left on the outside of the turn. The centre is rotating strongly to the right with contrary body movement travelling towards the inside of the turn. The feeling should be when rotating that the centre travels along the small circle and the head is travelling along the big circle. When maintaining this technique, you will perform a nice swinging action to the natural turn and the head weight will counterbalance your partner's.

Half of a natural turn moving backwards four, five, six for the man one, two, three for the lady. Stepping backwards and rotating to the right, with head weight to the left, the partner is travelling around you. This is where the lady's head stays in one place. In this case, the centre travels along the big circle, and the head travels around the small circle with almost no movement. This allows the partner to pass easily and maintains counterbalance.

Half of a reverse turn moving forward steps one to three for the man and steps four to six for the lady. When dancing the reverse turn they are different; both partners are extended to the left and this must be maintained. When stepping forward and turning to the left, the head weight is towards the centre of the turn and this should also be maintained. The head will be travelling along the small circle. The centre is travelling around the partner along the big circle. If you envisage your centre on this big circle moving diagonally forward, you will feel your right chest muscle rise upwards and over. This will allow you to perform the reverse turn more easily and without losing position.

Half of a reverse turn moving backwards steps four to six for the man and steps one to three for the lady. Stepping backwards and rotating to the left, with head weight to the left and will be on the outside of the turn. The head will be travelling along the big circle, your centre will travel along the small circle and is on the inside of the turn. Pay attention to the head on the big circle and by keeping it there you will allow for the power in the reverse turn.

This applies to all natural and reverse figures in all standard dances:

- tango natural twist turn
- waltz double reverse spin
- quickstep running right turn
- foxtrot closed impetus

The rules apply as above depending on whether going forward or backwards dancing natural or reverse figures.

PIVOTS

Pivots are a continuous rotation as a couple and they require specific foot positions, body positions, weight change and balance between the couple. A single pivot will have a 180-degree of rotation of the bodies of the couple around a common axis. While pivoting on the ball of the standing foot, there will be half a turn.

The partner moving forwards will have a step of heel toe, and is responsible for the spot of the axis and the momentum of the turn of the pivot. The foot that is stepping is in the contrary body movement position and this position indicates a clear right side lead. The swivel of the standing foot allows the couple to exactly exchange their positions, while moving down the line of dance. The partner that initially set the axis for the turn and the momentum of the movement will now be in a position to receive the position of the axis and momentum from the other partner to complete the next half of the turn.

The turn is made from the base with static connection at the top. Turning and creating momentum from the top will cause you to lose your balance. A vertical rotation around the common axis is essential. When stepping forward, the foot should be straight forward with the knee and thigh also straight forward. A slightly turned-in foot will maintain your weight centred but the knee and thigh should remain straight forward. A turned-out foot, even if only slightly turned, could make you overturn, lose balance or change the direction of the line that you wish to follow. When stepping backwards, the foot should also remain straight.

Make sure you have static balance and keep your knees soft. (Static balance has been described in the section Static in More Detail.) The legs should be held in position with your thighs connected to your partner, creating a solid base to perform the pivot. Keep the heel of the back foot off the floor at all times to avoid an abrupt stop and try not to tense the body, as this will unbalance the partnership.

Pivots need practice to establish the amount of power to put in. Too much power will not allow a

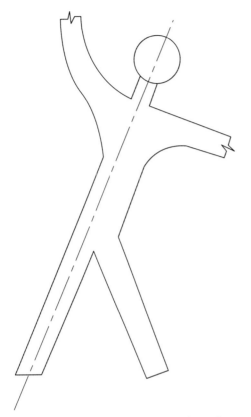

The sway is when the body leans away from the direction of travel to prevent falling over.

clear position change and too little power will not allow you to achieve a 180-degree turn. Responsibility for good pivots is equal between the couple.

SWAY

We use sway in ballroom dancing to stop the momentum that has been created by swing to stop, slow down or change direction. The faster you are moving, the more momentum you will create, so the more sway you will need. An example of this is a motorcycle – the faster it goes, the more the rider has to lean into the turn as they go around bend. So in dancing, the body is leaning away from the direction you are dancing too, to stop you falling over.

The spine will no longer be vertical to the floor but it should remain straight although on an angle. There should still be a straight line from elbow to

elbow with no distortions. Sway happens naturally and will be in proportion to the swing: this is called natural sway.

We also have sway that we manufacture to create bigger lines. This is done by tilting the shoulder line to exaggerate shape. This is achieved by stretching one side upwards, without making the opposite side break at the waist. Therefore, you will need to stretch this side, as well creating a feeling of an arrow going upwards from one side to the other. Do not try to use the arm to create the stretch. This stretch is added to the natural sway and is not meant to replace it. This kind of sway was not used in ballroom dancing a decade ago and shapes were less exaggerated and more controlled. For example, this is done between steps two and three of the natural turn in the waltz: when the feet are closing, the man should stretch his left side and the lady the right side in an upward direction; there should be no distortion of the straight line from elbow to elbow, so any use of the arm to stretch will create distortion.

We also have broken sway, which is a bending to the side from the waist; it is only used in lines and you do not move your feet, e.g. the oversway. Broken sway should never be used in moving figures, such as the natural turn in the waltz, and should not substitute natural sway. Natural sway is used in all steps that have swing. Manufactured sway can make technical sway look more attractive.

SWING

Swing is the action of moving the leg from the hip in either a forward or backward direction.

Pendulum Swing This occurs when we swing a whole leg or the entire body like a pendulum in a clock. Swing is produced from a high position to a low position. Lowering produces the swing down and then we have the driving action creating energy to rise upwards. The characterization of the waltz is a pendulum swing but it also can be seen in the quickstep and today can be seen in foxtrot as well.

Rotary Swing   This occurs when we allow rotation to generate movement. An example of this is when someone is throwing a hammer in sporting events: once the thrower stops rotating, the hammer is let loose and continues to move.

Metronomic Swing   This is a forward tilt of the top part of the body to create movement. An example of this is all runs out of the promenade position in the quickstep.

Combination Swing   Most figures have a combination of swing. An example is the natural turn in the waltz. Commencing to move metronomic swing, lowering to drive, downward pendulum swing, rotary swing begins at the end of step one, rotary and upward pendulum swing work together to rise up and sway will slow down the swing.

THE USE OF RISE

Rise and fall, swing, and sway are all connected in some way. Without the correct rise and fall, we cannot build our swing, and without correct swing, sway cannot be achieved. Rise and fall happens throughout our dancing, so it is important to have a good knowledge of it if you want to improve the look of your dancing and the feeling between the partnership.

The use of the ankle joint by extension and flexion is what is known as foot rise. Rising up on to the ball of the foot is called foot rise. Examples are when rising up on to a toe, as in heel toe, toe, and toe heel toe. When it is stated 'toe heel' or 'flat', there will be no foot rise. For example, the natural turn in the waltz: on step one for the man he will rise up on to the ball of the foot at the end of his step before he takes step two; the lady, however, has no foot rise until step two – this is because the lady is on the inside of the turn and has to allow for the man to swing past before she can rise up.

In the foxtrot feather step, again the lady does not have any foot rise, so here she will now use her legs and body to rise up. To allow this to happen, the lady will not have any flexion of the knees and hips,

but the knees are never locked out. The man will be rising up through his feet.

Body rise is achieved by lengthening the spine. This is achieved by using the transverse muscles, which gives a feeling of pulling the lower back backwards or thinking of pulling the belly button to the back of the spine, which lengthens the lower back. Pulling the chin in at the same time results in a lengthening of the whole of the spine. So, by connecting the leg rise with the body rise, the result will be that we are much taller.

We have now covered the three types of rise: foot rise, leg rise, and body rise.

Leading.

LINE POSITIONS

Same Foot Lunge Position

In the same foot lunge position, the lady's hips are not parallel to the man's. The lady's left hip is placed on the man's right side in front of his right hip, while she is facing the man's right side. The man will lead the lady by slipping his hips beyond the lady's turning her to the right This position is also used in a right hinge.

Hinge Position

The hinge position is where the lady's hips are perpendicular to the man's. The lady will be in a position facing the man's right side and her hips will sit on the left side of the man's hip.

LEADING

To have a good lead, it is essential to have a good frame, good posture and good balance. The lead must come from the leader's centre of gravity, the torso, which is connected to the frame. The man's frame must be consistent so that the lady feels secure and aware of where the man is. The man must not lead with his arms – the arms move in response to the body and base; if the man tries to lead with his arms, then he will be either pulling or pushing the lady and the lady will feel that she has no control over her own movements. The distance from the man's centre to the palm of his hand should never change. The man should not pull his hand in or extend it out and away from the lady. He should never dance into his own hand, as this would mean that he kept his hand still but moved his body into his hand. The hand moves because the body moves, so the distance remains the same. A good exercise to try is to imagine that your arm is in plaster and therefore cannot move in or out, and neither can the body move into it. The man's right elbow should always be in front of his chest and not behind.

Having achieved a strong frame, the man only needs to use his base and his arms will move forward without him moving them, and the lady will feel the base move and move accordingly. If the man pushes with his arms, the lady will be forced to move to catch her own body weight. If the frame stays still and the distance between the man's centre and palm of the right hand stays fixed, the lady will glide along easily and be able to transfer her own weight.

Another way to understand this is to imagine using a shopping trolley. When we shop we do not pull and push the trolley in and out by moving our hands in and out. We normally keep the same distance between the trolley and our arms from the elbow to the hand, and we don't walk into our arms.

Following.

It will be your base that is moving the trolley and the arms are staying still.

FOLLOWING

Following is not as easy as it sounds and certainly it is not possible to sit back and go along for the ride as long as the man is a very good dancer. Following is an art and should not to be taken lightly. It is often suggested that the lady should be submissive to her partner, who is the leader, and he who must be obeyed. Ladies – do not underestimate the role of the lady dancer. This is very much not the case and undermines the expertise of some of our lady dancers who are experts of their craft. Having had the chance to watch and admire many top ladies dancing, and recognizing their amazing ability to follow, it is without any doubt that a good lady dancer is a vital component to an equal partnership. So ladies, do not be blasé while dancing – acquire as much knowledge as possible and be active in finding solutions to the problems that may occur in the partnership.

We have mentioned, in the Viennese waltz, how to dance backwards and that the movement is initiated by the person going forward. It is the motion of the partner moving forward that guides the partner moving backwards, so here is a good example of the lady initiating the forward movement. Following requires the lady to be receptive, not submissive, responding actively to leads from the man.

As a beginner, it is unreasonable to expect the lady to be able to respond in the same way as an experienced dancer but we hope that we have given enough information for you to be able to respond to some of the signals from the man. The lady should maintain a right-side connection and not move across the partnership unless the step dictates it. The lady should try not to pre-empt the step that the man is going to dance or expect him to stick to the routine. So she should wait to feel the signal from the man as to what he would like to do and then respond actively. If you are social dancing, then you will be dancing with many different partners, so you will not be familiar with their routines or how they dance.

If the man is dancing like a bull at a gate, the lady has no chance of waiting and trying to feel a signal from the man, as she will just be pushed off her foot. With no signal, she has no chance to respond, so in these instances, the lady needs to speak up and point out what she may be feeling.

When first learning to dance as a couple, the man may give several signals all at the same time and this can confuse his partner, so this is a process that the couple need to go through until progress is made. Thinking of the steps, timing, footwork and choreography is enough to contend with, and on top of all of this, we have to learn to pick up and feel signals from our partner.

A simple feeling for the lady might be when the man turns his body to the left or the right, the lady's body will respond accordingly, turning to the opposite side. When the man turns his body to the left, the lady will turn her body to the right. When the man turns his body to the right the lady will turn her body to the left.

Commencing to take a step, the lady should feel that she receives a signal from the man that comes through his flexing of the knee and the pelvis moving forward, which will give her the feeling to move. She will then feel him continuing his lowering action and will continue to lower herself. The weight should be transferred from one foot to the other and, hopefully, this will happen smoothly together. The lady must not commit her weight to her moving foot before the man. A good exercise to do is to reverse the roles and see how it feels to do each other's role.

ISOLATION

Isolation is the movement of one part of the body independently of the rest. One part of the body does its own movement, so when initiating contrary body movement, only the top part of the body moves, the hips stay where they are. If the hips move as well as the body, then there will be no contrary body movement. The hips should be able to move independently of the ribs. The head should remain still when turning the body underneath it; if the head turns as well as the body, we are dancing as a block, which is incorrect. The body rotates underneath the head – when this occurs it may look as though the head has moved but it has not. The head moves on its own in certain steps. The dancer needs to be able to point the hips in one direction, while the ribs are in another direction.

ROTATION

Moving Rotation

In some steps, we are rotating at a certain point

Torque rotation is when we twist the body to accommodate a direction of movement.

in the step to prepare to step outside our partner or to initiate a turn. The most common is contrary body movement. When preparing to step outside our partner, we rotate the upper body slightly to be able to move outside but stay connected to them. For example, let's take the feather step: at the end of step one, the man turns slightly to the right with his upper body to step outside his partner, as well as continuing the forward movement. The lady also turns her upper body.

Circular Rotation

Circular rotation is when both partners turn around a central point. For example, the double reverse spin, natural top and the standing spin. There are two forces acting on the bodies: centrifugal force pulls the bodies apart, while centripetal force creates energy towards the centre of the turn. An example of this is the hammer throw: the faster the person turns, the easier it is to turn because of the centrifugal force and when the hammer is released, the centrifugal force sends it flying off.

During most circular rotations, in which two bodies are joined together, one of the partners is on the outside of the turn while the other is on the inside of the rotation. The partner on the outside experiences centrifugal force and the one on the inside experiences centripetal force, which will become easier with increased rotation. To stay connected to our partner during circular rotations, the partner on the inside needs to keep their centre towards their partner. Another example is the natural spin turn: the man creates centrifugal force through the circular rotation in the initial pivot, his action is then converted to a moving rotation, while the lady begins with a moving rotation and then a circular rotation over her left foot.

Torque Rotation

Torque rotation is used when we twist the body to accommodate a direction of movement. For example, the chase in tango: in this step, the man uses moving and torque rotation to be able to step around the lady.

A routine that is made up of a combination of

rotational steps could be in the tango: chase followed by a fallaway whisk and pivots. The chase involves moving rotation and torque rotation, as the man uses contrary body movement and torque to be able to step around the lady. Circular rotation happens in the fallaway whisk when the man is at the centre of the turn, while the lady dances around him. The man then has to apply torque rotation at the end of his whisk to be able to keep his centre towards the lady. The lady should be aware that if she moves too quickly, she might open to promenade before the man gets a chance to apply his torque rotation.

These forces can destroy the beginner's steps as well as advanced steps, so it important to understand them. It would be useful to evaluate your routines to see which of these rotational forces are being used. If either partner is unaware of these forces, a mistake can pull the couple apart.

Pivots involve circular rotation in which the partners change from the inside and outside of the turn. To make the pivots smooth, the partner moving backwards pulls to the inside of the turn, creating centripetal force, which assists the partner generating centrifugal force. The roles are then reversed, so both partners have to work equally for good pivots to be danced.

BEWARE FOOTWORK MISTAKES

We have discussed footwork in the earlier chapters of this book but you might encounter footwork that might be slightly different from what is usual. Having described what would be 'normal' footwork, we will now cover footwork that you might not be dancing correctly.

Quickstep

For example, rumba cross in the quickstep as a man, which curves to the right around the lady, similar to a forward lock, which has exaggerated shape and rotation. It is a very advanced figure, but many dancers do not realize that the man's first step should be taken as a heel toe, as a first step of a lock step is usually danced on a toe; with the second step, the man crosses behind, so it seems unusual that a lock step should commence on the heel. It is danced in this way because of the exaggerated shape of the rumba cross. This step begins low and shapes strongly to the man's left, and that is the reason it is danced on the heel. After the step is taken, the man begins to rise and shape to the right allowing him to roll from the heel to the toe.

TANGO

Reverse Turns
Open Reverse Turn lady outside
Open Reverse Turn lady in line
Basic Reverse Turn

These three steps are danced by placing the second step flat, which will allow for more stability and ease, instead of dancing without lowering the heel.

FOXTROT

Back Feather
Wave for the Man

Ladies dance a feather step or a three step as toe heel on each step, but many men may not know that when they are going backwards they should dance. Step one, toe heel, step two, toe, step three, toe heel, which will give the correct rise and fall.

In the Bounce Fallaway the lady should dance the first step toe heel toe. Step two is on a toe, because of the man's rise which the lady should match.

CHAPTER 8

MUSICALITY, FLOOR CRAFT AND ROUTINE CONSTRUCTION

MUSICALITY AND PHRASING

Musicality is more than just being on time. It is about making your dancing fit the music and matching it to the music that is being played, even though you may not have heard it before.

Beats of music that are grouped together make up a bar, and these bars grouped together make up phrases. There are eight bars to a phrase and the phrases grouped together make up a full piece of music. Beginner dancers listen to the beat at first until they are more proficient at their dancing. Advanced dancers need to learn to listen to when the bars and the phrasing come, and not all bars of music are the same. Fitting your dancing to the beats and the differences among the bars of music is what phrasing is.

Correct phrasing will create powerful dancing within the phrase. Perfecting good musicality will help you dance well within the bars. Beats one and three are the most powerful beats of music in each bar and we need to emphasize them; for example, the first beat in the foxtrot is the driving step, while beat three has a feeling of holding.

MUSICALITY IN TANGO: STACCATO VS. LEGATO

Tango is seen as a sharp, fast and explosive dance with no swing and sway. A good tango should be danced with contrast and interpret-ation of the music. It can be danced slowly and smoothly or sharp and fast. Interpretation of tango

Musicality in tango.

music can be explained in staccato (sharp), which means disconnected in Italian – there is a pause between each note. Legato (smooth) means bound together in Italian – there is no pause between the notes and the notes run into each other. When using a staccato action in dancing tango, the foot should be placed on the floor quickly and remain there for the rest of the beat, while the body moves over and the next step is taken. The body does not move with the foot that is being moved and the back foot comes from behind to end in front. The body moves because of the leg action and, although the feet are staccato, the body is not, as this would produce a jerky type of movement.

Legato is a much smoother action and the feet are not placed so sharply; the foot can slide along the floor as in a stalking action. Legato can be expressed in the body by slowly turning to the promenade position with the upper body.

It is possible to mix staccato and legato action in your routines. Use a staccato action to close promenade and legato on a progressive link or vice versa. There is no hard-and-fast rule but try not to use the same action for more than two bars of music. Dancers who have been dancing for a long time learn to use the actions to fit the music that is playing, which will lend itself to both staccato and legato.

FLOOR CRAFT

Types of Floor Craft

Learning floor craft is important in order to be able to dance around the floor without bumping into other couples. Learning to change routines and adjusting the alignments will help us to maintain a flow around the floor. Alignments can be curved, so as not to have to change the routine. If it is not possible to curve, then a line figure could be danced as they are easy to get out of.

Pivots are useful as they do not generally affect the routine too much. Pivot until you are back on the same alignment.

Steps can be changed for other steps but the man

has to have extensive knowledge of the steps and be able and proficient at leading them.

Examples

Waltz:
- On making a natural turn and planning to follow it with a spin turn, you find you are blocked from dancing down the line of dance. Instead, dance a closed impetus, which has the same amount of turn but does not travel as far down the line of dance.
- On dancing steps one to three of a reverse turn, you had planned to continue down the line of dance but you are blocked. Dance a reverse corte or hover corte, then a back whisk, which could be continued with the promenade position and curve the next figure.

Foxtrot:
- You are planning to dance a reverse turn and wish to dance a feather finish but there is congestion down the floor on the line of dance. Dance instead a reverse turn, under turn steps one to four, so that the man ends backing the diagonal wall, then dance a basic weave, ending on the same alignment.

Tango:
- When planning to dance an open reverse turn diagonal to centre, you are blocked. Dance a progressive side step reverse turn, ending on the same foot with less space needed.
- You are planning to dance a walk or progressive link to the diagonal wall, but a couple have moved in front of you. Dance instead a back corte moving to the side or to the left.

Quickstep:
- When planning a quick open reverse diagonal centre, you are blocked. Dance a fishtail, allowing you to check the movement and then continue on the same alignment.
- You are planning to dance back locks down the line of dance but there is not enough space. Dance a running finish, moving around any couples.

HOW TO CONSTRUCT A STANDARD ROUTINE

When constructing a standard routine, breaking it down into three main parts should provide a good understanding:

- Structure
- Design
- Musicality

STRUCTURE

Negotiating the dance floor can be overwhelming and seen as difficult but broken down into the above parts should make it relatively easy. We'll start with structure, which means putting together a routine of figures that enables dancing around the floor efficiently.

When building a routine, try not to take it around the outside in the shape of the floor being danced on. It should be taken along the floor, towards the centre of the floor, into the corners and out towards the centre again. Remember not to dance across the centre line of the floor as this will be dancing into oncoming dancers, so stay on your own side. Not all routines are structured in this way and it is possible to allow for changes within this structure. Rotational figures to the right can be danced in the corners as well as a line figure. Moving down the floor, progressive figures can be used.

DESIGN

When designing a routine, it will need what is called light and shade, which means, soft and strong and differences in the timing using syncopation. So rotation, progression, spins and lines are needed to make up an eye-catching routine.

Progression is travelling down the line of dance with power and speed. To take advantage of this it is best danced down the long side of the floor.

Some figures that travel (in other words, ones that progress down the floor):

- Waltz: progressive chasse to the right, weave from promenade position, turning lock to the right.
- Foxtrot: reverse turn and feather finish, reverse wave, bounce fallaway with weave ending.
- Quickstep: natural turn and back lock, quick open reverse, six quick runs.
- Tango: open reverse turn lady outside, basic reverse turn, the chase.

Rotation

These are figures that rotate. Rotation is ideally suited for the shorter couple who perhaps cannot demonstrate progression down the line of dance as well as a taller couple with long legs. Strong rotational figures are also just as eye-catching as progressive ones. Pivots are very well suited across the whole of the short side of the floor. Down the long side of the floor, dancing figures that turn to the left, which are reverse turns, can be used.

Some figures that are rotational:

- Natural figures:
  - Waltz: natural spin turn, outside spin, left whisk.
  - Foxtrot: foxtrot does not have many rotational figures as it is a linear dance, so strong rotation is not normally used, but the foxtrot does have figures that turn to the left and the right that are not strongly rotating.
  - Quickstep: natural spin turn, running right turn, rumba cross.
  - Tango: natural promenade turn, pivots after oversway.

- Reverse figures:
  - Waltz: double reverse spin, open telemark, fallaway reverse and slip pivot.
  - Foxtrot: fallaway, reverse and slip pivot.
  - Quickstep: reverse pivot, double reverse spin, closed telemark.
  - Tango: oversway, fallaway reverse and slip pivot.

- Line figures are when we hold a position for one or two bars of music to allow for extension and shaping:

- Waltz: hesitation change, left whisk, hover corte (the hover corte is a strong line figure and can be held for longer to increase the stretch and shape).
- Foxtrot: change of direction, natural hover telemark.
- Quickstep: hover corte.
- Tango: back corte, contra check, oversway.

Note that waltz hesitation change, tango back corte, and foxtrot change of direction and natural hover telemark are in themselves line figures but may be danced with exaggerated shaping to give the appearance of a line figure.

MUSICALITY IN A ROUTINE

Musicality is when dancing coincides with the music. A musical phrase is made up of eight bars of music and each phrase should match the routine being danced. The strongest beat in the phrase should match a powerful step, e.g. in the waltz beat one and step one of a natural turn. Working on phrasing can make dancing look more attractive and stronger. When dancing corresponds with the music, it is what is called musicality.

The hardest part of building your own routine is where to start, so here are some suggestions on how to do this:

- Waltz: natural spin turn starting at the corner of the beginning of the long side. The man should be facing the diagonal wall, while the lady is backing the diagonal wall.
- Foxtrot: feather step starting just out of the corner of the long side. The man should be facing the diagonal centre, while the lady is backing the diagonal centre.
- Quickstep: natural spin turn starting at the corner of the beginning of the long side. The man should be facing the diagonal wall, while the lady is backing the diagonal wall.
- Tango: open reverse turn, lady outside, starting near the beginning of the long side. The man

should be facing the diagonal centre, while the lady is backing the diagonal centre.

Example Routine Based on Intermediate-Level Waltz

Note that the distance travelled will be different from couple to couple, so you may need to allow for this and adapt your routine accordingly.

Figures

Starting at the beginning of the long side.

Natural Spin Turn Timing and Phrasing

Man facing the diagonal wall 123 223
Lady backing the diagonal wall

4 to 6 of a Reverse Turn

Man backing the diagonal centre 323
Lady facing the diagonal centre

Double Reverse Spin

Man facing the line of dance 423
Lady backing the line of dance

Progressive Chasse to the Right

Man facing the line of dance 52&3
Lady backing the line of dance
Can also be danced
Man facing the diagonal centre
Lady backing the diagonal centre

Back Lock

Man backing the diagonal wall 62&3
Lady facing the diagonal wall
Corte or hover corte, then a back whisk, which could be continued with promenade position and curve the next figure.

Back Whisk Turned to the Right 723

Man backing the diagonal wall
Lady facing the diagonal wall

Chasse from Promenade Position

Man moving down line of dance 82&3
Lady moving along line of dance

123 Natural Turn
Man facing the diagonal wall 123
Lady backing the diagonal wall

Open Impetus
Man backing the line of dance 223
Lady facing the line of dance
You have now reached the corner of the long side of the floor.

Weave from Promenade Position
Man moving to the diagonal centre 323423
Lady diagonal centre
Wing from promenade position
Man facing the line of dance 523
Lady backing the line of dance

Progressive Chasse to the Right
Man facing the line of dance 62&3
Lady backing the line of dance

Back Locks
Man backing the diagonal wall 72&3
Lady facing the diagonal wall

Outside Spin
Man backing the diagonal wall 823
Lady facing the diagonal wall

You are now in the corner at the end of the short side ready to begin again.

DANCING MUSICALLY

Dancing musically is when the sound of the music is transformed into a visual expression, when music is movement. To make the dancing more musical, the timing is played with, and we try to feel the music. We can make the 'slows' slower with the 'quicks' quicker and use the same amount of time in a bar of music, so that we do not go off time, we just change it slightly.

For example, in the waltz natural turn, we can hold the two count longer as if suspended in the air and have less time on the three count. We are stealing time from the previous beat or the one that follows. When dancing one step to one beat we are being proficient but not musical, we want the dancing to represent the character of the music, and to flow with the music, to interpret the music when slow and at other times when it becomes fast. When the music has a crescendo, so should our dancing. To dance musically requires skilled dancing and is an art that can be aspired to.

Visual expression of dancing musically.

CHAPTER 9

EXERCISES AND NUTRITION TO IMPROVE YOUR DANCING

Before beginning the exercises, I would like to mention here the benefits of yoga, tai chi, the Alexander technique and training with weights. All four of these disciplines have served me well in my dancing. Yoga is a good exercise for flexibility, strength and bone loading, as well as posture, poise and balance. Tai chi is good for feeling, strength and balance. Weight training is good for strength, stamina and bone loading. The Alexander technique is excellent for balance posture, poise and many other benefits.

ALEXANDER TECHNIQUE

The Alexander technique was first introduced to me through my yoga teacher and I found it very beneficial to my posture, movement and dancing. It can help with muscular tension, aches and pains created by constantly tensing up the muscles in an attempt to move, dance and trying to execute complicated choreography when not on balance or in control of body weight. It will help you to pay attention to posture and the alignment of the spine in a very simple and relaxing way.

The Alexander technique was first invented by Frederick Matthias Alexander in Australia at the end of the nineteenth century. He concluded that the body could have perfect posture, balance and poise with little or no tension, and that many activities and functions could be improved.

Try to become aware of where you may be holding tension in the body, especially in the neck, and try not to contract the neck muscles while dancing. Think of the shoulders moving away from each other, rather than pulling the shoulder blades together, which can affect the neck, and also pull the elbows backwards. When lengthening the spine, try not to brace it, thereby causing stiffness, as this works against ease of movement. The result that is required is strength and the ability to move efficiently and comfortably.

All information about the Alexander technique can be found online. There are Alexander technique practitioners available if you would like to work on the technique.

Please be careful when you exercise so as not to cause yourself any injury. If you have any medical or physical impairments, please check with your doctor before you start these exercises. If you have not previously done any exercise on a regular basis, it is advisable to start off very gently, especially if you are doing them at home on your own with no instructor or trainer.

1. Lie down on the floor with your legs outstretched and your arm by your sides. If you feel any discomfort in your back, lie with your knees up. Stretch your arms over your head to touch the floor behind you. Bring your arms back over to your sides.

Repeat this exercise ten to twenty times. It would be advisable to start with five, building up slowly to ten and so on.

This is a basic stretch to help with stretching the whole body.

2. Still lying on the floor, bring your knees up, keeping your feet on the floor. Your arms should be stretched out to the side. You should be aiming to keep your shoulders on the floor at all times. Take your knees over to the right very carefully, and then bring them back to the centre and then over to the left.

Repeat this exercise ten to twenty times, building up from five and so on.

This exercise will help with your contrary body movement position and when you need to turn to the left or right; also in trying to isolate the hips from the ribs.

3. Sitting on a chair, turn your body to the right and then to the left. First, hold the right knee with your left hand and turn to the right. Next, hold the left knee with the right hand and turn to the left.

Repeat this exercise twenty times, starting with five and so on.

This exercise also helps with contrary body movement position, and turns to the right and to the left.

4. Stand against a wall with the back of your heels touching the wall and stretch your arms above your head to touch the wall.

Repeat ten to twenty times, starting at five and so on.

This exercise helps with stretching the whole body before the next exercise.

5. Still standing against the wall with your feet about a foot away from the wall, try to bend forwards to touch your toes – do not force anything. You should be trying to stretch upwards and forward as you begin to go down, and try not to collapse the body. Try to keep the legs straight and do not bend the knees. There is a feeling of the bottom sliding up the wall.

Once again, repeat ten to twenty times, starting at five and so on.

This exercise helps with stretching the hamstrings and calves.

6. Stand in front of a chair with your feet shoulder-width apart and have your feet about two to three inches in front of the chair, with your feet facing forward. As if you were going to sit down, try to get to a squat position, keeping the feet facing forward. Keeping your back straight, start to squat down to sit on the seat. Do not bend too far forward and stick your bottom out, but you should feel a slight forward stance. It might be helpful to take the arms forward to help with balance. You should feel the muscles in your thighs working and not any pressure in the knees. Try not to collapse on to the chair but to control the weight and lowering action, and just touch the chair and rise up again.

Repeat this ten to twenty times, starting with five and so on.

This exercise helps strengthen the legs.

7. Find a fairly thick book that will allow the heels to lower to the floor – not too thick to start with. A block that you can purchase from a sports shop can also be used and these blocks are very useful. Rest the ball of the foot on the book, then rise up and lower the heels down until reaching the floor. Do not try to use the body to heave yourself up, try to use only the foot. If this is difficult, try holding on to a wall or something else.

Start with ten repetitions, building up to twenty.

This exercise helps to strengthen the calves and ankles, and also stretches the calves and the Achilles' tendons.

8. This next exercise is a very advanced stretch, so please do not try it unless you are confident that you are aware of the degree of difficulty or that you have spoken to your gym, yoga or exercise teacher.

Lie on the floor with a foam roll or a large, rolled-up towel that fits the width of the shoulders and is positioned just below the shoulder blades, about where a lady's bra strap would be. Now lie over it, start with the knees bent and then try to straighten your legs carefully. Support your head with a cushion or rolled-up towel if your head does not touch the floor. Lie in this position for a few minutes, increasing the time as the body begins to stretch.

This exercise is good for the lifting of the ribcage for both man and lady, and also helps the lady a great deal in her extension when dancing and taking hold. This exercise will also help with posture and poise. It is a good exercise for correcting any over-curvature of the thoracic spine area.

Many ladies today may believe that extension is achieved by leaning backwards from the lower back. This is not the case, although it may very well look like this when watching very good dancers. If the lady leans backwards from the lower back she will be back-weighted and unbalanced. This can cause back pain and even injury over time.

The lady extends backwards from just below the shoulder blades, which lifts the front of the ribcage. Added to this is a slight rotation and lateral movement.

It might be useful to add here that in today's dancing, rightly or wrongly, some of the line figures are being danced with an exaggerated backward bend from the lower back. Whether this is just a new fashion or will be the start of things to come is a question of time.

9. Sit on the floor with your back straight. You can position a foam block at the base of your spine for support and to stop you slouching forwards. Spread your legs open and, reaching upwards towards the ceiling with both arms, start to move forward a few inches and hold this position for a short time. Continue to stretch forward and start to move downwards as far as you can manage. The aim of this exercise is for the head to reach the shins and the chest to the knees. Do not bend or round the back to achieve this result, but keep reaching forward and downwards, and eventually the body will be able to reach the required position. Project your body forward from the ribcage. To help in this action, keep stretching your arms upwards and forward. Try to take your chest to your thighs, not your head to your knees.

This exercise helps stretch your groin, as well as increasing your flexibility. It can also be performed with the legs outstretched and together.

EXERCISE FOR BALANCE, POSTURE AND STRENGTH: TREE POSE

This exercise is derived from the yoga discipline and it will strengthen the legs and the core muscles. It will also improve balance and posture. It is well worth taking the time to work on this exercise.

1. Begin by standing up with the feet together.

2. Transfer the weight on to the right foot. Bend the left knee up and open the leg out from the hip to the left.

3. Place the bottom of your left foot on the inside of the right thigh or shin (make sure that it is not on the knee to prevent damage to the knee). If you find this difficult, you can keep the ball of the left foot on the floor but still open the leg out from the hip. Place the heel on the inside of your right ankle and calf area with the toe pointed to the floor.

You may want to do this standing sideways to a wall, with the standing leg next to the wall. This will help if you lose your balance. Do this exercise on both legs.

When performing this exercise, the hands come together with the palms facing each other in a prayer position at chest level, with the elbows up and the forearms parallel to the floor. Lengthen down through the tail-bone and draw your shoulders down the back. Fold the shoulder blades in towards each other and pull the navel to the back of the spine.

Having attained proficiency with this exercise, you may want to try raising the arms above the head, keeping the palms together. This requires more balance and strength.

Pull the navel to the back of the spine and feel the stretch throughout the body and the lifting of the ribcage.

CORE EXERCISES

To obtain a strong core stability, which is essential to the dancer, you need to exercise a variety of

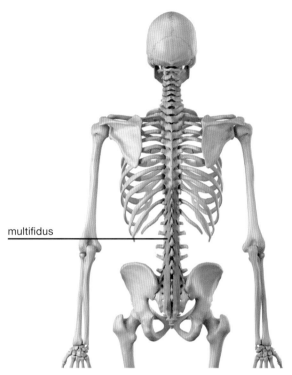

multifidus

Multifidus muscles that need strengthening for core strength. SHUTTERSTOCK

muscles from the hips to the shoulders. It is thought that core strength is just having a nice six-pack (rectus abdominis), but this is not the case. Core strength consists of a variety of muscles that run the length of the torso. When these muscles contract, they stabilize the spine, pelvis and shoulder girdle. Therefore, for core strengthening, all of these muscle groups need to be effective.

- Rectus abdominis: front of the abdomen known as the six-pack (see the photograph in section Posture of Chapter 2).
- Erector spinae: running down each side of the spine from the neck to the lower back.
- Multifidus: these are under the erector spinae along the vertebral column; they extend and rotate the spine.
- External obliques: located on the side and front of the abdomen (see the photograph in section Posture of Chapter 2).
- Internal obliques: under the external obliques and run in the opposite direction.

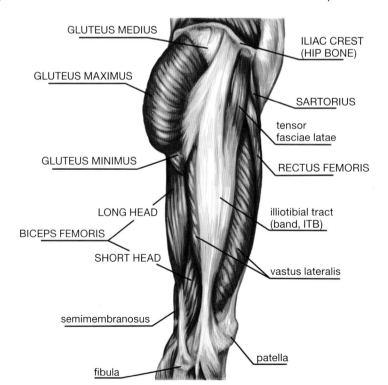

GLUTEUS MEDIUS

ILIAC CREST (HIP BONE)

GLUTEUS MAXIMUS

SARTORIUS

tensor fasciae latae

GLUTEUS MINIMUS

RECTUS FEMORIS

LONG HEAD

illiotibial tract (band, ITB)

BICEPS FEMORIS

SHORT HEAD

vastus lateralis

semimembranosus

patella

fibula

Gluteus medius and minius and piriformis. Muscles that need strengthening for core strength.
SHUTTERSTOCK

- Transverse abdominis: these lie under the obliques and are the deepest of the abdominal muscles. They wrap around the spine like a corset for stability and protection (see the photograph in section Posture of Chapter 2).
- Hip flexors: these are in front of the pelvis and upper thigh and include the psoas major, the illiacus, the rectus fermors, pectineus and sartorius.
- The gluteus medius and minius: located at the side of the hip.
- The gluteus maximus: hamstring muscles, piriformis located at the back of the hip and upper thigh.
- Hip adductors: located mid-thigh.

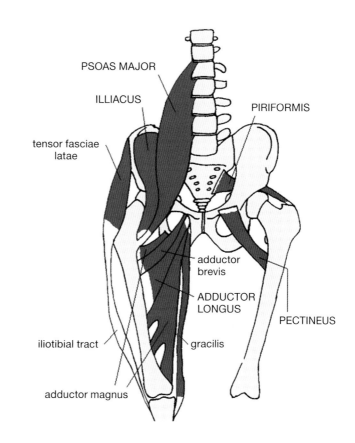

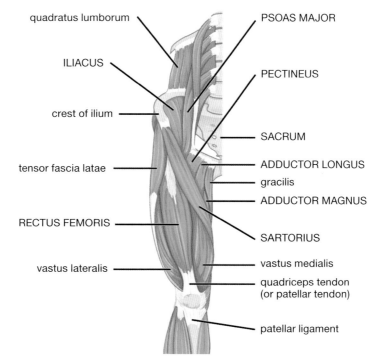

TOP RIGHT: **Psoas and illiacus. Muscles that need strengthening for core strength.**
BETH OHARA/WIKIMEDIA

RIGHT: **Hip flexors. Muscles that need strengthening for core strength.**
OPENSTAX COLLEGE/
WIKIMEDIA

The benefits of core strength include:

- Reduces back pain.
- Improves performances.
- Improves posture.

There are many exercises to strengthen the core muscles; we have chosen the following ones for you to start off with.

The Plank

This exercise engages all the muscles that make up the core and is a good one to start with. Lie face down on the floor and bring the arms in front with the elbows at chest level. Raise the chest off the floor, to simulate the sphinx position. Turn the toes over so as to be balanced on or near the ball of the foot. Pull the core (tummy) muscles in and the pelvic floor muscles, so that you are now balanced on the arms and toes in a plank position. Keep the body straight from the ears to the toes.

The Bicycle

This is a good exercise for the rectus abdominis and obliques.

Lie flat on the floor on your back, making sure that the back is into the floor and not concaved. Place your hands behind your head. Bring the knees up to a 45-degree angle, ready to perform a bicycle pedalling action – as if riding a bike, we have one leg up and one leg out. If riding a bike one leg is bent up and one is down. First, touch the left elbow to the right knee and then the right elbow to the left knee. Perform this slowly and in control about ten to twenty times on each side.

The Bridge

This is a good exercise from yoga that strengthens your gluteus muscles (buttocks) and hamstrings (back of thighs).

Lie flat on your back with the knees bent, arms by your side, palms facing down. Tighten all of the core and pelvic floor muscles. Raise the hips towards the

The plank exercise. SHUTTERSTOCK

The bridge exercise. SHUTTERSTOCK

ceiling, feeling the chest moving towards the chin. Hold this position and then repeat. If this is the first time of performing this exercise, then hold for twenty seconds and build the time up to two minutes. This exercise can also be performed with an exercise brick that is placed under the lower back after you have raised your hips up, to help you understand the position and gain strength.

The Twist

This exercise is good as it engages the upper and lower body, as well as the core muscles, in a fairly easy movement. It is a good exercise to perform as a warm-up prior to dancing.

Walk forward and swing both arms across the body to the opposite knee that is rising upwards. Raise the knees as high as is possible. This exercise can also be done skipping instead of walking. Skip or walk ten strides forward, increasing the strides

as fitness improves. This is also a good exercise for performing, and fitness for, the quickstep.

The Boat

Another yoga exercise to work the rectus abdominis, external obliques, internal obliques, and hip flexors.

Sit on the floor on something that is soft or cushioned. Contracting all your abdominal, core and pelvic floor muscles, raise the legs up to a 45-degree angle. At the same time, reach forward with straight arms out in front of you towards the knees and shins. Hold for a few seconds and repeat five times, increasing as you get stronger.

The above exercises may be challenging but are definitely worth persevering with. If exercise has not been part of your routine, you will be using muscles that you have not been used to working, but if you

The boat exercise. SHUTTERSTOCK

go slowly and perform them regularly, they will get easier as your muscles get stronger.

With perseverance the snail reached the ark!

SOME WARMING-UP AND LOOSENING EXERCISES

The following exercises I personally found beneficial from my tai chi classes.

1. Stand with your feet shoulder-width apart, raise the arms to shoulder height in front of you and let them drop down towards floor, to the sides of your body, while at the same time bending your knees as the arms drop, then swing your arms back up to the starting position.

Repeat this twenty to fifty times.

2. Stand with feet shoulder-width apart, take your right arm up to shoulder height and turn the right side of the body forward, then drop the right arm down. As you are dropping the arm down, begin to take the left arm and the left side forward. When the arms are dropping down, flex the knees and bend. It's the flexing of the knees that drop the arms down; feel gravity taking them down.

This exercise can help you with using your right and left side.

These are just two of the exercises I have chosen to warm up with. There are many beneficial exercised in tai chi that will help you with your dancing if ever you would like to take it up. It's amazing.

Lunges

If you have been fortunate enough to go to a gym, you will have done lunges at some point. These are not only a very good exercise for strengthening the legs, but very good for warming up to dance.

Step forward with the right leg with the foot facing forward, standing now in a split leg position. The feet should be about three feet apart, which can be increased as you become more proficient. Turn the toes of the left foot slightly outwards. Lunge forward into the right foot but try to keep the body back as if someone is pulling you back. Do not let the knee go forward to end over the toes; there should be a straight line from the knee to the toes. Don't lean back; you should stay in the middle of your legs, Try to go as low as you can but be careful – you should not feel it in your knees and groin. Now change legs. Perform between twenty and fifty, increasing slowly.

Exercises for the Achilles' Tendons

Dancing puts a lot of pressure on your legs and feet and inevitably on your Achilles' tendons. The Achilles' tendon is the largest tendon in the body and stretches from the calf muscles to the bones in the heel. It can withstand a lot of use but can be injured through overuse leading to tendonitis. Warming-up exercises to stretch the tendon are advisable.

1. While sitting on a chair, raise your toes as high as you can to the point where you can go no higher. Slowly lower your toes. Repeat this exercise up to twenty times.

This exercise can also be done standing up and is also a strengthening exercise for the ankles.

2. Stand facing a wall with your hands on the wall, feet together, and take one leg back about a stride. Bend the front knee and straighten the back leg, lowering the heel to the floor. This will stretch your calf and the Achilles' tendon to a point where you

feel a strong pull. You don't want to go to a point where it becomes painful. Hold this position for fifteen seconds and then repeat on the other leg.

Repeat up to twenty times on each leg.

Exercises for the Ankles

1. Sitting on a chair, take one foot off the floor and start to draw a circle with the toes only – make the circle as large as you can. The shin should remain still.

Repeat this exercise slowly twenty times, then reverse the action circling the other way.

This exercise will help strengthen the tendons and the muscles around your ankle. This is also a very good warming-up exercise to do before starting your dancing.

2. Stand with the feet together and rise up on to the toes and lower slowly.

Repeat twenty times and try to increase as the ankles get stronger.

3. Physiotherapists may use a resistance band, which is an elastic band that can be obtained from a sports shop. Using the band around the ankle and performing flexing and pointing, everting and inverting the ankle slowly and with control, helps to strengthen the small muscle groups around the ankle.

KEEPING THE FEET HEALTHY

Keeping the feet healthy by preventing a problem is better than curing a problem bought about by neglecting the feet.

Bunions can be a major problem to dancers – this is when the big toe joint is pushed out to the side and the toe is angled inwards towards the other toes. This can be an extremely painful condition, making it difficult to walk and even more difficult to dance. Shoes also become a problem to fit. Surgery is sometimes needed to resolve a bunion.

Wearing tight-fitting and pointed shoes that squeeze the toes together can cause you to get bunions. So when choosing your dance shoes, make sure that they do not squeeze your toes together and cause pain. There are shoes with a more rounded toe that may suit you better but also make sure that they are not too tight.

The tendon that runs from the ball of the foot to the heel is called the plantar fascia and this can become inflamed and will cause pain in the heel. This condition can become serious and cause micro-fractures. To prevent this happening, stretching can be of help. As the plantar fascia is connected to the Achilles' tendon and into the calf, the following stretching exercises will be beneficial to all three.

1. Standing on a stair on the balls of the feet, and holding on to the banister, lower the heels downwards.

2. Sitting on the floor with one leg straight and the other bent, so the foot is facing the thigh of the straight leg, place a belt around the extended foot and pull the toes back towards you. Repeat the same on the other leg. Pulling the toes back, and not just the ball of the foot, the plantar fascia will be stretched.

Dancing in high heels can shorten the calf muscles, so they need to be stretched as well, and would benefit from performing the above exercises.

NUTRITION FOR DANCERS

Nutrition for the dancer may not seem important when first starting to learn to dance, as you may feel that you are not really using up a lot of energy. It is something, though, that should be given some thought, as you will be using different muscles if you have been sedentary and not used to exercise. Although your specific needs can only be determined by a professional dietician, some basic knowledge can be helpful.

Muscle is important and we can lose muscle mass very easily if we do not eat enough protein, as protein maintains and builds muscle. So even though we are not trying to be Mr Universe, we still need good muscle tone to stay on our feet and have the strength to perform any kind of physical activity.

The body can only process between 20 and 25g of protein at any one time. Having three meals a day that contain some form of complete protein will help you obtain enough protein. Trying to eat too much protein will not be beneficial, as the excess protein will be converted to sugar. At the end of this topic a more scientific way of working out how much protein we need will be explained.

The B vitamins are important for releasing stored energy. It is not possible to have too many B vitamins, as they are water soluble and any excess is excreted in the urine.

Iron helps the red blood cells carry oxygen around the body and is especially important for cardiovascular endurance.

There are two sorts of carbohydrate: complex ones and simple ones; both are sugar. Simple sugars will be released into the bloodstream very quickly; these are found in cakes, sweets, chocolate and sugar that you put in drinks. Some of the complex ones are rice, pasta and bread, and these have to be broken down by the body and are released at a much slower rate. Complex carbohydrates are converted by the body into glucose and used for energy. The complex ones are released at a much slower rate than the simple ones, which go directly into the bloodstream. It is important to have enough carbohydrates before you exercise so that the body has enough fuel to carry out the demands of physical exercise. Two hours is a good time to have carbohydrates before you start exercising or dancing. Do not eat large meals just before starting your exercise, as the stomach will be full and the body will struggle to digest the food and cope with exercise at the same time; being sick may be a consequence of this.

Fat is required by the body in order to function. Fats provide energy and absorb fat-soluble vitamins A, D and E, and help store these vitamins. Fats save protein from being used for energy, allowing protein to do its job of repairing and building muscle tissue. Good fat protects the heart. It is the bad fat that increases the risk of heart disease. Unsaturated fat is the good fat found in olive oil, avocados, almonds, Brazil nuts and salmon. Mackerel, kippers and sardines provide omega 3. Some bad saturated fats are fatty meat, cheese, cream, biscuits, cakes, palm oil and coconut oil; try to avoid these fats. Cutting out all fat from the diet is detrimental to health, so stick to the good fats.

Equally important is that the body recovers well after exercise, or your dancing practice, so we need to consume some good nutrients. This can be made up of protein, carbohydrate and water. A protein shake can take the place of a meal, if preferred. Very vigorous and continuous exercise can also deplete the body of electrolytes, so a good electrolyte drink will help with this. Make sure that you eat soon after you have finished exercising, but not directly after – waiting twenty minutes is beneficial.

If you are dancing for a long time, don't forget to sip water throughout.

An Example of How Much Protein to Have in the Diet

The National Institute of Health recommend 0.36g of protein per 0.45kg of body weight for a sedentary person; other sources differ. An easy way to calculate is 1g of protein for 0.5kg of body weight:

- Height 168cm, female, 40 years, weight 60kg, lightly active with a sedentary job. Approximate amount of protein per day: 105g.
- Height 173cm, male, 40 years, weight 70kg, lightly active with sedentary job. Approximate amount of protein per day: 131g.

Please note this is an approximate guide and you should check with a health practitioner or look on the internet if you are in any doubt about your protein intake.

If you are exercising, running, walking, biking, swimming and dancing, this is not considered lightly active and so your protein intake may need to be much more.

If we are not getting enough protein for our requirements, the body will hold on to its fat stores and use the protein we eat for energy so body mass is lost.

CONCLUSION

'Countless unseen details are often the only difference between mediocre and magnificent.'

Author unknown.

'*Festina lente*' a very dear departed friend used to say to me, which has great meaning: 'hurry slowly'.

MISUNDERSTANDINGS AND ARGUMENTS IN DANCING

Arguments occur in everyday relationships, so will also occur no doubt in dancing. Gaining knowledge can prevent a lot of misunderstandings and arguments. Learning both the man's steps and the lady's steps can be a great advantage and can help to correct steps that are going wrong. If both parties understand where their partner should be and how to do the other's steps, it will avoid any guesswork from the other partner as to who is at fault. It is useful for the lady to know how it feels to lead and for the man to experience how to follow.

If a partner thinks it is easy to follow, then experiencing it will reveal that it is just as difficult as leading. A partner believing that they were not led correctly, so therefore could not follow, may want to check themselves out first to see if they may be part of the problem. Also, the partner leading who thinks that their partner is not following, may want to look at what they might be doing to cause the problem.

Listening to our partner can be difficult if there is a feeling of being criticized or blamed. Try to pinpoint the problem or what you may be feeling without making it the other person's fault. Words have different meanings to different people and misunderstandings occur; asking your partner for an explanation of what they might mean may help. Both partners should respect one another's opinion, whatever their standard might be. People bring different skills to a partnership and, even if they are not as advanced as their partner, their skills in other areas may well be of importance that can help with the dancing. Guard what you say so as to avoid either insulting, hurting or bullying a partner.

WHAT TO LOOK FOR IN A PARTNER

What to look for in a partner? First, do not rush into any partnership. A quotation that has a calming effect is 'what's for you, will not go by you'. Look for similarities and differences to see if your aspirations are the same or similar. Trying to find a partner who is of a higher standard than yourself is not necessarily a bad thing, as long as they are not too far advanced from your own standard. A partner below your own standard might prove to be very useful, as with lessons they can catch up quickly.

Lessons are important, so check out if they want to have lessons and who with and how many they would like – weekly ones or monthly – and how many you would like to have. You may already have a teacher that you go to and would like your partner to go as well. Check out what goals they may have and if they coincide with your own. Talk about how you will practise and where, and if travelling is a problem. Find out if they are dancing socially or if they want to be more dedicated than perhaps you want to be. They might be too dedicated and want more lessons and practice than perhaps you had in mind.

THOUGHTS ABOUT LEARNING TO BALLROOM DANCE BY CHRISTINA CREMIN

It is often believed that a crash course on ballroom dancing will be enough to make one competent to navigate a dance floor. Booking a cruise led to an 'absolute beginners' six-week dance course, in order to dance on a social floor on our cruise. Unfortunately, after two crash courses, we still stumbled about nervously on a crowded dance floor. Now, six years later, we have discovered there is no quick route to make fast progress and we were naive to believe we could.

Taking up a new discipline has its rewards, and when my husband and I took it up, we were two people at the same level, it was good fun learning together. It keeps the brain working and the body moving and it is a really lovely feeling when you have mastered enough steps to be able to dance around the floor. There is a sense of pride and satisfaction that all your hard work has paid off.

With ballroom dancing it is entirely up to the individual the standard that they wish to achieve; whether to dance for social pleasure or to take their dancing to a higher level, or maybe to do competitions. It helps if both parties have the same ambitions.

What we found was that many classes were available to teach steps but it was difficult to find a teacher willing to show you how to dance the steps correctly with the correct technique. If you are lucky enough to find someone willing to teach you more in-depth, it makes a massive difference to the look and feel of your dancing and, although harder, it is much more rewarding.

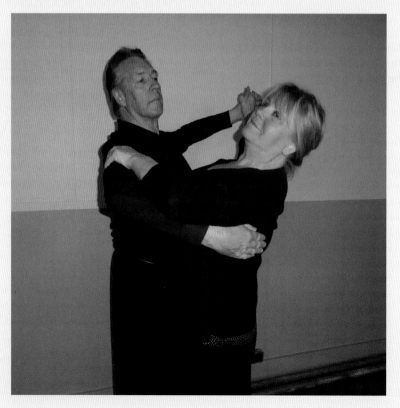

Fortunately, we found this teacher very early on before too many bad habits had formed (so thank you Janet for all your patience and the effort you have put into helping us with our dancing).

When good dancers make the dancing look easy it gives the impression that it is not difficult to do, but when you try yourself to emulate them, you can appreciate that even after six years, you are still a beginner.

Christina Cremin.

Dance etiquette.

DANCE ETIQUETTE

Dance etiquette is nothing more than good manners and common sense. On the dance floor, we should behave in the way that we would expect others to behave towards us. Having the proper etiquette ultimately helps everyone to fit in together and avoid conflicts with other dancers.

Please be aware of your personal hygiene and the clothes you are wearing. Anything but dance shoes is still considered not generally acceptable. Gentlemen, wearing shorts as opposed to long trousers, is still frowned upon. If you are prone to perspiration, consider wearing multi-layers of clothing and taking a change of clothes.

The Golden Rules appertaining to the dance floor are:

- Do not walk across the middle of the dance floor and do not carry food or drink on the dance floor. If you spill anything, do mop it up as quickly as you can.
- Do not presume to put talcum powder or the like on to the floor to even out a sticky floor, without asking the organizer's permission. This could, at worst, cause an accident and is difficult to clean off. Also, water can ruin the floor.
- Ladies should use heel protectors and certainly not dance with stiletto heels, as these could damage the expensive floors.
- It has always been seen to be the prerogative of men to ask the ladies to dance. However, today it is not inappropriate for a lady similarly to ask a man to dance. It is good manners to thank your partner after the dance.
- Always dance along the line of dance in a counter-clockwise direction. Do not stop to have a conversation with your partner or other dancers on the dance floor. Do not dance against the line of dance for obvious reasons.
- Do not practise your steps on a social dance floor and do not dance a different dance to the music that is being played.

Inevitably, on a crowded floor there will be some bumping into other couples. When this happens offer a polite apology. Remember everyone is sharing the dance floor and no one exclusively owns it. It is helpful and advisable to adjust arm positions to avoid bumping into other people. Practise good floor craft.

Above all – enjoy yourself! That is what dancing is all about.

Hopefully you will find this book helpful and if willing to travel the path uphill will find the gold at the end of the rainbow.

INDEX